Gender and Politics

Series Editors
Johanna Kantola
University of Tampere
Tampere, Finland

Sarah Childs
Birkbeck, University of London
London, UK

"There is simply no other book that combines a practical knowledge of what gender training looks like on the ground with an academic knowledge of the hopes and critiques that have been laid on it. I found it highly readable, appropriate for the mixed audiences of academics, activists and entrepreneurs to which it is addressed. Any reader will be convinced that Ferguson has been listening to their experiences with training and their critiques of it."

—Myra Marx Ferree, Alice H. *Cook Professor of Sociology, University of Wisconsin-Madison, USA*

"This book is a welcome and timely addition to the existing literature on the theory and practice of training for gender equality. Its accessible format and style mean it will be extremely useful for trainers and training commissioners wishing to reflect more deeply on their practice and enhance the impact of training for gender equality."

—Clemencia Muñoz-Tamayo, *Chief of UN Women Training Centre, Santo Domingo, Dominican Republic*

"In an effort that is long overdue, this book pushes beyond the academic critique of gender mainstreaming to explain what 'feminist gender training' looks like. Grounded in feminist theory and methodology, and based on a deep familiarity with policy and training practices, it intelligently assesses the transformative potential of gender training while engaging with its critique. This is a highly satisfying foray into a topic that has deeply divided feminist academics and practitioners."

—Elisabeth Prügl, *Professor and Director of Gender Centre, Graduate Institute of International and Development Studies, Geneva, Switzerland*

The Gender and Politics series celebrated its 7th anniversary at the 5th European Conference on Politics and Gender (ECPG) in June 2017 in Lausanne, Switzerland having published more than 25 volumes to date. The original idea for the book series was envisioned by the series editors Johanna Kantola and Judith Squires at the first ECPG in Belfast in 2009, and the series was officially launched at the Conference in Budapest in 2011. In 2014, Sarah Childs became the co-editor of the series, together with Johanna Kantola. Gender and Politics showcases the very best international writing. It publishes world class monographs and edited collections from scholars—junior and well established—working in politics, international relations and public policy, with specific reference to questions of gender. The 15 titles that have come out over the past five years make key contributions to debates on intersectionality and diversity, gender equality, social movements, Europeanization and institutionalism, governance and norms, policies, and political institutions. Set in European, US and Latin American contexts, these books provide rich new empirical findings and push forward boundaries of feminist and politics conceptual and theoretical research. The editors welcome the highest quality international research on these topics and beyond, and look for proposals on feminist political theory; on recent political transformations such as the economic crisis or the rise of the populist right; as well as proposals on continuing feminist dilemmas around participation and representation, specific gendered policy fields, and policy making mechanisms. The series can also include books published as a Palgrave pivot.

More information about this series at
http://www.palgrave.com/gp/series/14998

Lucy Ferguson

Gender Training

A Transformative Tool for Gender Equality

palgrave
macmillan

Lucy Ferguson
The Graduate Institute of
International and Development
Studies
Geneva, Switzerland

Gender and Politics
ISBN 978-3-319-91826-6 ISBN 978-3-319-91827-3 (eBook)
https://doi.org/10.1007/978-3-319-91827-3

Library of Congress Control Number: 2018941883

Printed on acid-free paper

This Palgrave Pivot imprint is published by the registered company Springer International Publishing AG part of Springer Nature
The registered company address is: Gewerbestrasse 11, 6330 Cham, Switzerland

For Leo and Rudy

Acknowledgements

First, I would like to acknowledge the support of the UN Women Training Centre in funding the Working Paper Series on Training for Gender Equality which provided an opportunity to reflect on some of the key questions addressed in this book. Next, I thank the wonderful Ruya Leghari for her razor sharp editing work and always insightful comments. To my Tier 1 for keeping me creative, grounded and buoying me up. Finally, big thanks to Ken for all the support and allowing me the space to follow my passion in getting this book written.

Contents

List of Figures

CHAPTER 1

At the Intersection of Theory and Practice: Locating Gender Training

Abstract This book explores how to maximise the transformative potential of gender training scenarios and processes. It does so by highlighting and interrogating innovations from practice in order to overcome some of the key challenges for gender training. The book constructs a notion of *feminist gender training*, which is reflexive, self-critical and focused on process. This chapter traces the historical development of the field of gender training, drawing on a range of resources and projects that have attempted to map the emergence and current state of gender training. It then goes on to map the field of gender training and explore how processes of professionalisation and developing quality criteria can contribute to a more feminist-informed theory and practice of gender training. This chapter establishes the book's explicit focus on transformation, which sets it apart from the more technocratic aspects of gender training. Moreover, it asks how gender training can be harnessed as a catalyst for disjuncture, rupture and change.

Keywords Mapping gender training · Professionalisation · Quality criteria · Transformation · Feminist gender training

This book is concerned with the possibilities and limits of gender training as a transformative tool for gender equality. The term *tool* has been selected in order to firmly locate gender training within a broader set of practices and processes for gender equality across a range of

L. Ferguson, *Gender Training*, Gender and Politics,
https://doi.org/10.1007/978-3-319-91827-3_1

levels—institutional, societal and individual. Gender training has often been dismissed as overly technical and devoid of political content (Mukhopadhyay 2013). Indeed, this may be a fair reflection of much of what passes for 'gender training' in contemporary institutions and organisations. However, I hope to reclaim optimism for what gender training can do and argue that it is a vital part of any change process towards gender equality. Of course, it is important to recognise the limitations of gender training. Yet even while doing so, it is possible to strive for gender training to be ever more feminist and ever more political. As such, this book serves as a contribution to discussions about what can and cannot be done through gender training, located within broader conversations about the possibilities for feminist change in institutions, societies and individuals.

Before going into these debates in a substantive manner, it is useful to first develop a working definition of gender training that will guide the conceptual and practical foundations of this book. For example, the UN Women Training Centre—based in Santo Domingo—offers the term 'training for gender equality' as opposed to gender training, with the aim of broadening the scope of what such training can achieve. Training for gender equality is defined as:

> A transformative process that aims to provide knowledge, techniques and tools to develop skills and changes in attitudes and behaviours. It is a long term continuous process that requires political will and commitment from all parties involved (both decision makers and trainees) with the objective of creating an aware, competent and gender equitable society. (UN Women Training Centre, n.d.)

This notion of a 'transformative process' is particularly useful for the focus and approach of this book. As noted in a review of gender training since the Fourth World Conference on Women, held in Beijing in 1995 (UN Women Training Centre 2015b), gender training has been referred to in diverse ways since the establishment of 'gender mainstreaming' in the 1990s, as shown in Fig. 1.1. The review notes that these terms have often been used interchangeably, and there is little conceptual clarity on the differences and similarities between them. Moreover, this varies by sector or Critical Area of Concern in the *Beijing Declaration and Platform for Action* (PFA).

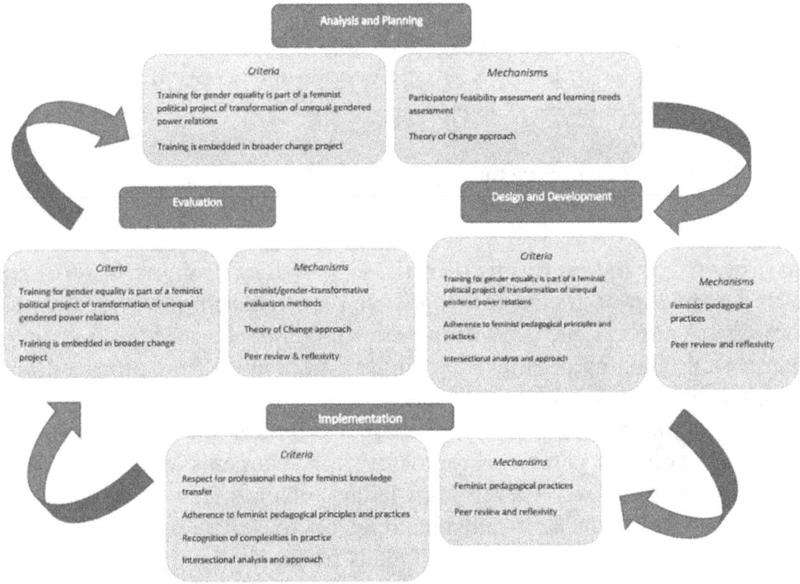

Fig. 1.1 UN Women Training Centre approach to integrating quality criteria and mechanisms across the training cycle (*Source* UN Women Training Centre (2017b))

Box 1.1 Focus of gender training across the PFA's critical areas of concern

In some areas, the focus of training is predominantly on skills training for women—namely poverty, the economy and the environment—without an explicit discussion of the role of training in gender mainstreaming within these fields. Other areas—notably education and the girl child—are concerned with non-discrimination training. In the remaining Critical Areas of the PFA, greater attention is given to 'gender-sensitive training', more closely in line with the approach of this book. The sections on health, violence and human rights particularly highlight the need for gender-sensitive training for personnel. In the sphere of Institutional Mechanisms for gender equality, the proposed measures include staff training in designing and analysing data from a gender perspective, alongside training and advisory assistance to governments, in order to help integrate a gender perspective in their policies and programmes.

Source UN Women Training Centre (2015b).

In order to expand on this further, the UN Women Training Centre produced a *typology* of gender training in 2016, establishing five key themes: awareness raising and consciousness building; knowledge enhancement; skills training; change in attitudes, behaviours and practices; and mobilisation for social transformation. Training geared towards raising awareness and building consciousness "introduces participants' to key issues concerning gender (in)equality and women's empowerment," while training centred around knowledge enhancement "provides more in-depth information and understanding on these issues and the power structures underlying inequalities." Skills training enhances competences related to gender. Training to elicit change in attitudes, behaviours and practices "fosters lasting positive changes in the way participants think and act, as well as their long-term habits." Finally, training that aims at mobilisation for social transformation "stimulates participants' capacity to collaboratively put their knowledge, motivation and skills into practice, in order to change their work, communities and daily lives into more gender equitable spaces" (UN Women Training Centre 2016: 6). In essence, distinguishing between 'types' of gender training is important, the Training Centre argues, to help "set realistic objectives, pick appropriate modalities, use effective methods, cater to the needs of audiences, and select suitable trainers " (ibid.: 6). Nonetheless, they acknowledge that—at its core—what really matters is *process*. For instance, the Typology notes that "different types of training are not mutually exclusive [….] Nor are they meant to imply a chronological process of learning, where awareness is followed by knowledge, then skills, and change in attitudes, behaviours and practices, and finally, social transformation. Effective learning is an ongoing and continuous process in which 'learning' is more usefully understood as a 'circle' or 'cycle', not a linear trajectory" (ibid., 2016: 11). The discussions included in this book draw on analytical concepts such as Training Cycle—a key analytical tool for exploring the different processes and power dynamics of gender training—and gender training modalities.

What is important to highlight from this brief review of definitions or types of gender training is that the key concern of this book is with the *process* of gender training, as opposed to the specific content or context in which it takes place. Moreover, many trainings overlap in terms of their form and objectives. As such, it is perhaps more useful to consider the underlying premise of all gender training to be social transformation. In order to achieve this, different types of training can be conducted in different modes and contexts. However, in order to be an effective *transformative tool for gender equality*, gender training must be guided by a series of processes, principles and practices. These are developed in more detail throughout the book.

This concern with gender training as a transformative tool for gender equality in institutions and public policies worldwide is located at a critical juncture of growing interest in transformative change processes (Krook and Mackay 2015; Caglar et al. 2013; Bustelo et al. 2016c; OPERA Team 2011; Hoard 2015). At the same time, the field of gender training has continued to grow and is now a widely deployed tool for implementing gender mainstreaming strategies and gender equality policies worldwide (see, for example, the UN Women Training Centre's Community of Practice and the European Institute of Gender Equality's (EIGE) Gender Trainers Database, as discussed below). Despite this dual growth—both in terms of a field of academic research and of practice—there is currently no academic publication specifically dedicated to the current state of gender training. This book aims to meet two pressing needs, already identified in the literature and practice on gender training: first, the need for more research on the theory and practice of gender training (Bustelo et al. 2016a); second, calls for the sharing of tools and strategies for overcoming practical challenges in gender training (UN Women Training Centre 2015a).

In sum, the book offers a critical analytical review of the theory and practice of gender training, with an accessible format that encourages and supports readers to develop pragmatic solutions to the prevailing challenges and tensions in the field. The objective of this introductory chapter is to provide an overview of the field of gender training, setting the context for the following chapters which address more substantive questions. The chapter is developed in three main sections. The first draws together work on gender training to offer a picture of the **current state of the field**. Attempts to cultivate a professionalised field are mapped here, such as the UN Women Training Centre Community of

Practice and the EIGE Gender Trainers Database. The second part of the chapter involves a discussion of attempts to develop **shared professional criteria**, and the dilemmas and tensions raised by such processes. A number of such initiatives are discussed: the 2011 Madrid Declaration on Advancing Gender+ Training in Theory and Practice; the 2006 Gender Manifesto; the UN Women Training Centre's 2017 Working Paper and Virtual Dialogue on Professionalisation; and the 2017 UN Women Training Centre's Certification Course and its Quality Assurance Criteria. These different approaches are critically analysed and contextualised within a broader discussion of professional ethics for gender training and gender experts, following Prügl (2016). Finally, the third section of this chapter sets out the **aims and overall approach**; structure and format; and key themes and arguments of the book. The discussions in this book are guided by one overarching question: what can be done to maximise the potential of gender training to contribute to feminist processes of transformative change?

Gender Training and Gender Mainstreaming

The roots of gender training as defined above can be largely traced to the emergence of 'gender mainstreaming' following the 1995 Beijing Conference. However, arguably gender training also has its foundations in consciousness-raising workshops of the 1970s and 1980s, an important part of the feminist movement's engagement with women's experiences and struggles, and its questioning of how to connect these to broader structures of patriarchy, capitalism and other systems of oppression (Bustelo et al. 2016b). As set out above, in this book I am concerned with gender training as part of a broader process of transformative change for gender equality. The relationship between gender training and gender mainstreaming is discussed in detail in Chapter 3. Here the focus is the historical development of the field of gender training, drawing on a range of resources and projects that have attempted to map the emergence and current state of gender training.

In order to locate the origins and development of gender training, it is useful to turn first to UN Women Training Centre's (2015b) review of gender training since 1995. This paper begins by analysing how gender training was addressed in each of the review periods since Beijing, undertaken once every five years. At Beijing +5 in 2000, training was featured frequently in the UN Secretary-General's Report on advances in gender equality since the Beijing Conference. Noted achievements included a number of countries introducing awareness-raising and gender awareness training in an effort to change institutional culture in public sector agencies and departments. The concluding section of the +5 Report calls for the expansion of gender training. By 2005, progress had been made on resource allocations for training, and a wide range of training activities had been conducted for government institutions, civil society, women's organisations and individual women. In terms of Area H—Institutional Mechanisms—during this period, governments were urged to promote gender training for both women and men in government ministries. Several states instigated training on gender-sensitive budgeting. Responses from countries in all regions included information on capacity-building workshops and training programmes. As such, the Beijing +10 review revealed that training had become a widespread tool for gender mainstreaming by 2005. Indeed, in several of the Critical Areas of Concern of the Beijing Platform for Action, this was the peak period for gender training activities (UN Women Training Centre 2015b).

By the third review of Beijing in 2010, Beijing +15, training featured strongly in the reports and analysis. The Secretary-General's Report concluded that many national machineries had expanded their capacity development and training functions for all members of government; the availability of gender mainstreaming tools had increased—including guidelines, checklists, manuals and guidance for conducting gender impact assessments; and that specialised training, workshops and seminars had been provided for staff in ministries and government agencies, including for senior managers. Finally, in the most recent substantive review—Beijing +20 in 2015—training was discussed primarily in relation to the PFA's Critical Areas of Concern. The most detailed reflection was in relation to Institutional Mechanisms. The Secretary-General's Report outlined that some countries had developed training to strengthen staff skills in gender analysis. However, it also noted—as in previous years—that staff capacity in national gender equality machineries, limited by a lack of training and investment, remained a key challenge to implementing the Beijing PFA (ibid.). Alongside this analysis, the UN Women Training Centre's paper offers a number of key findings and recommendations regarding the development of the field of gender training since 1995, as shown in Boxes 1.2 and 1.3, respectively.

Box 1.2 Key findings of the UN Women Training Centre's review of gender training since Beijing 1995

- Training has been an important tool for increasing gender equality, and has flourished substantively, beyond the original expectations set out in the Platform for Action.
- Despite the proliferation and institutionalisation of training for gender equality in many areas, there is a concerning lack of information on the impact and evaluation of such training.
- The development and institutionalisation of training for gender equality has been uneven across different Critical Areas of Concern.
- Training for gender equality since Beijing has not always addressed the structural aspects and power relations which perpetuate inequality.
- The provision of training for gender equality has often involved collaboration between different actors, expanding beyond a focus on the public sector to encompass the private sector, civil society and numerous other key players.
- While training for gender equality has developed, evolved and expanded consistently since Beijing, there appears to have been a decline in focus on training and a reversal in its scope in recent years.

Source Adapted from UN Women Training Centre (2015b).

Box 1.3 Recommendations of the UN Women Training Centre's Beijing review

- Raise awareness of the important role played by training for gender equality in increasing equality between women and women since the Beijing Conference.
- Continue to develop adequate systems for the monitoring and evaluation of training for gender equality in order to measure outcomes and impact more systematically.
- Explore the possibilities for expanding training for gender equality in Critical Areas of Concern which have received less attention to date.

- Promote the value and role of training for gender equality as a tool for transformation in gendered power relations.
- Encourage collaboration between a range of actors to expand and enhance the provision of training for gender equality while supporting the UN to be a world leader in this field.
- Work to reverse the trend of a declining focus on training.

Source Adapted from UN Women Training Centre (2015b).

As such, the development of gender training has taken place in parallel with the growth of gender mainstreaming worldwide. Gender trainers and gender equality actors seized the windows of opportunity opened at different levels and scales—international, EU and national or domestic levels—in order to embed gender training within the expanding regulation and institutionalisation of gender equality (Lombardo and Forest 2012; Kantola 2010). However, as argued by Bustelo et al. (2016b: 7), this potential has not been fully realised and gender training remains a "highly contextual, weakly institutionalized activity, which is developing at a different pace across geographical areas and policy sectors, and involving a multi-faceted range of actors." Moreover, gender training has been exposed to the same challenges and setbacks as gender mainstreaming more broadly, as set out in more detail in Chapter 3.

Mapping the Field of Gender Training

Other projects have aimed to map not just the settings and areas in which gender training has taken place, but also who have been the actors involved. That is, who are the gender trainers? The OPERA-QUING and TARGET projects, for example, explored the "diversity of legal and policy settings for gender training," highlighting the "considerable variety of actors and approaches involved in gender training activities" (ibid.: 8). One of the key activities of the OPERA-QUING project was a conference in Madrid in February 2011, which brought together nearly 140 gender trainers, commissioners and experts from a range of fields, including gender and development, justice, post conflict management and policy design and implementation. The conference led to the Madrid Declaration on Gender+ Training, as discussed in detail below. At the

EU level, the 2013 study *Mapping Gender Training in the European Union and Croatia* explored the profiles of gender trainers, drawing on the EIGE database. The study found that two-thirds of members of the database were affiliated with a private company, an NGO or a university, while the majority held higher degrees in a range of disciplines. Individual pathways to becoming a gender trainer were varied. While many trainers had pursued higher degrees in gender studies, this was very much country specific. The field of expertise also shapes the careers of gender trainers. For example, international development has been one of the most active fields for developing the methods and tools of gender training worldwide.

More recently, the Graduate Institute in Geneva conducted an extensive mapping exercise of 188 gender experts worldwide, in which gender trainers were a large part of the sample (Thompson and Prügl 2015). Its survey found that, of all expertise surveyed, 92% have graduate degrees, 72% had PhDs (mostly in social sciences, with very few in gender/women's studies), 60% self-reported as 'feminist', while 40% did not; and participants primarily reported that their knowledge on how to integrate a gender perspective was gained from their place of work. Although this survey was not explicitly targeted at gender trainers, but rather *experts*, 79% of whom worked for the UN, it helps to give a flavour of the field of gender training.

In summary, the field of gender training has developed substantively since 1995. Some form of gender training programme can now be found in most public institutions and across a wide range of sectors. Yet, to date, there has not been a comprehensive study conducted on the provision of, and participation in, gender training worldwide. We do not know, for example, who provided these courses, who these participants are, how many people have taken part in gender training courses and what the impact of such courses has been. However, the emerging field of research on gender training and gender expertise allows us to understand some of these questions, albeit in a sporadic manner. In order to explore these questions more substantively, I now go on to explore attempts at professionalisation in the field, which help us understand who is delivering training and the conditions under which training is designed and implemented. This analysis is revealing as it highlights some of the key tensions and challenges within the contemporary theory and practice of gender training, as discussed in more detail in Chapter 2.

Professionalisation and Quality in Gender Training

At the global level, there is no single organisation that coordinates the professionalisation of gender training as a field. This section addresses three key questions in order to explore this further. First, what professionalisation initiatives exist to date, where are they located and what kinds of groups or institutions have instigated them? Second, what kinds of values or standards might form the basis of a more professionalised field of gender training? Third, what are the key tensions involved in further professionalising the field and moving towards more standardised forms of certifying gender trainers? Debates regarding the professionalisation of gender training raise questions regarding the 'coloniality' of gender and gender training as a normalising technology, as discussed in more detail in Chapter 2. Nevertheless, it is useful to survey such initiatives here in order to contribute to a more detailed picture of the contemporary field of gender training. Moreover, it is interesting to explore how processes of professionalisation and developing quality criteria can contribute to a more feminist-informed theory and practice of gender training.

Top-Down and Bottom-Up Approaches to Professionalisation

Current initiatives can broadly be categorised into two kinds of approaches—top-down and bottom-up. In terms of top-down initiatives—that is, those initiated by national governments or international organisations—at the national level both France and Sweden have taken steps to formalise the field of gender training. In Sweden, a national certification system for gender equality consultants has been established, in which the expertise and experience of individual practitioners is reviewed and approved. Nevertheless, the field remains loosely structured and regulated, with the majority of firms and individual practitioners not certified under this process (Olivius and Rönnblom 2017). The French Women's Rights Ministry established a working group in 2013 on minimum quality criteria in gender training. The aim was to produce a "national framework, as well as a public label for gender trainers, while bringing together public and private expertise, academic and practical knowledge, and sharing views between practitioners and commissioners." To date, this has not yet been fully established.

Nevertheless, this move has triggered discussions across the field of gender training regarding the adoption of quality standards (Bustelo et al. 2016b: 7). Similar efforts can be noted in Denmark, Germany and the United Kingdom. However, these have tended to focus on the sharing of experiences and providing resources, rather than concerted attempts to professionalise the field (OPERA Team 2011; EIGE 2013). As such, to date, there is no formal certification process for gender trainers operating at the national level in any country.

At the international level, the key initiative worth noting is the recent 'Professional Development Programme for Gender Trainers', jointly managed by the UN Women Training Centre and the Royal Tropical Institute (KIT), the Netherlands. This programme emerges from several years of background work by both organisations, including a Virtual Dialogue on professionalisation (October–November 2016); a UN Women Training Centre Working Paper on Quality, as discussed in more detail below (UN Women Training Centre 2017b); and a KIT background paper on professionalisation (Wong et al. 2016), which offers a comprehensive review of professionalisation initiatives to date. Building on this work, the six-month certified programme aims to

> sharpen training skills and knowledge of gender and development concepts as a gender equality trainer; enable participants to better employ learning and knowledge strategies; support participants to re-claim training for gender equality as a political feminist process; renew participants as a gender equality trainer and their commitment to gender training as a transformatory process. (KIT and UN Women Training Centre 2018)

The course covers three main areas—conceptual depth and clarity, feminist practices and training skills and methods. It is aimed at gender trainers with a minimum of three years' experience and with knowledge of gender issues in relevant institutions.

Taken together, these initiatives at the national and international levels present a range of top-down approaches to professionalisation of the field. Bottom-up approaches—i.e. those which emerge out of collectives of practitioners and researchers working on gender training—are also interesting and merit discussion and reflection here. At the international level, the UN Women Community of Practice in Training for Gender Equality (CoP) can be understood as one such approach. Communities of practice refer to "groups of people who share a concern or a passion for something they do and learn how to do it better as they interact regularly" (Wenger 2007), with an "identity defined by a shared domain of interest." In such communities, they "develop a shared repertoire of resources: experiences, stories, tools, ways of addressing recurring problems—in short a shared practice" (Wenger 1998). The UN Women Training Centre's CoP aims to

> support the informed discussion and reflection on the current trends of training and capacity development for gender equality, the collection and dissemination of good practices and the identification of institutions, opportunities and resources for training for gender equality at the global level. The Community of Practice on Training for Gender Equality (CoP) provides an open forum for dialogue on new and emerging issues related to training and capacity development processes, as well as a platform for articulation and knowledge exchange between training for gender equality practitioners, gender equality specialists, and other key stakeholders from all around the world. (UN Women Training Centre 2018)

This Community of Practice includes Virtual Dialogues, Webinars, an Interview Series, an open discussion forum and resources on gender training, including a frequently updated database of upcoming training opportunities, a resource library of training materials and a database of institutions that deliver gender training worldwide. While ostensibly a 'bottom-up' approach to professionalising the field of gender training, the platform is nevertheless facilitated and moderated by UN Women. However, its content and exchanges are provided by CoP participants—that is, practitioners and experts in the field. As such, this is perhaps best described as an open Community of Practice that is supported and guided by UN Women Training Centre. In many ways, this institutional support is essential, as the background work required to moderate such a forum and encourage ongoing member participation is vital for a successful and sustainable community of practice.

Two further bottom-up initiatives can also be highlighted here. First, at the national level in Germany, the 2006 *Gender Manifesto* is concerned with the "danger of preserving, or even reinforcing, the mainstream gender order through Gender Mainstreaming and Gender Training." In order to overcome this, the Manifesto proposes a series of "theoretical and methodological premises and the standards for professional practice derived from them," with the aim of contributing to quality development in training and consultancy for gender equality. In terms of theoretical premises, they suggest making:

> a paradoxical approach to Gender the starting point for professional action; that is, to use Gender as an analytical category in order to overcome Gender as a classification category [or] using gender to undo gender. (Gender Manifesto 2006)

This involves using a 'three-step strategy', from construction to reconstruction to deconstruction, in order to "*make gender analysis itself the subject of the analysis.*" This strategy is outlined in detail in the Manifesto, along with five proposed criteria for professional practice.

Second, at a more international—although still arguably Euro-centric—level, the *Madrid Declaration on Advancing Gender+ Training in Theory and Practice* (QUING 2011) was developed in a collective manner at the OPERA Conference on Gender+ Training in Madrid in February 2011. The Declaration expresses a commitment to "delivering, commissioning and further developing the highest quality training." Using the term gender+, the Declaration acknowledges the fundamental importance of an intersectional approach to gender training—as discussed in more detail in Chapter 2—and sets out a clear notion of what such 'quality' entails. This relates specifically to different phases of the Training Cycle, covering positioning; content and methods; and the further development of training (ibid.). However, it is difficult to mobilise bottom-up approaches without consistent and sustainable institutional support and funding. As such, the Madrid Declaration has not been disseminated widely and has had a limited impact on the field and ongoing professionalisation processes.

Exploring the Foundations of Quality in Gender Training

In tandem with these efforts to professionalise gender training, discussions have taken place in a range of contexts regarding the ethical principles or normative standards that might underpin the practice of gender training. As noted by UN Women Training Centre (2017b: 4), "no consensus exists over what constitutes 'quality' in gender training, or what kinds of assurance mechanisms might be put in place for guaranteeing quality in this field." It has been argued that better quality training means better gender equality outcomes; that quality assurance may improve the process of commissioning training by giving trainers more legitimacy and voice in their negotiations with training commissioners; and that quality training is 'more likely' to contribute to transformation when it takes an 'inclusive, ongoing approach' to quality (EIGE

2014; UN Women Training Centre 2017b). Quality criteria and assurance mechanisms have been raised as a matter of concern by a range of actors and key stakeholders, including the Expert Group on Training for Gender Equality (UN Women Training Centre 2015a) and the European Institute for Gender Equality (EIGE 2014). Academic literature has also raised questions about the impact of the lack of quality criteria for gender training, such as the non-feminist characteristics of some gender work; the de-politicisation of feminist knowledge transfer; and the lack of a core set of ethical principles to guide gender training.

In addition to the Gender Manifesto and Madrid Declaration discussed above, two further approaches can be highlighted for discussion: the UN Women Training Centre's (2017b) working paper on quality and Elisabeth Prügl's (2016) work on professional ethics. This begins with a broader discussion of ethics, before moving onto a detailed look at the Training Centre's practice-focused approach. First, it is useful to outline in more detail what a set of professional ethics might entail for gender training, and for gender expertise more broadly. Prügl's work on this area is especially helpful, as she reminds us that "wielding feminist power requires ethical guidelines" (2016: 27). Taking a more conceptual approach, Prügl proposes a set of four key ethical principles for guiding the practice of gender training and expertise for gender equality, drawing on the fields of deliberative democracy and feminist methodology.

Box 1.4 Prügl's ethical principles for gender training

- Rational deliberation across difference that is open towards a change in being;
- Ensuring non-coercion and equality in deliberation, while enabling feminist social criticism;
- Inclusiveness of diverse knowledges paired with working in a participatory manner and, in partnership, for collective validation;
- Reflexivity *vis-à-vis* both processes and epistemic commitments.

Source Prügl (2016).

Prügl (2016) argues that rational deliberation is founded on understanding, requiring an openness to changing points of view and to changing the way we are. Such deliberation must be non-coercive, free from unequal displaces of power, and inclusive of diverse knowledges and participatory learning. Reflexivity is key, requiring an appreciation of the power relations in which we are embedded.

It is also important to acknowledge that in the practice of gender training, flexibility is required for dealing with resistances, tensions and conflicts—what Prügl refers to as "recognizing complexities in practice" (Prügl 2016: 38). This suggests an acknowledgement that, in some cases and contexts, a middle ground is required—between "embracing resistances and deliberation and delivering feminist expertise and training in less than ideal circumstances" (Bustelo et al. 2016a: 171). To quote at length:

> The purpose of gender expertise and gender training should be to make 'truths' on gender the subject of deliberation. In turn, this shifts the focus of feminist knowledge transfer from a primary concern with the 'quality of outcomes' to one which pays more attention to the 'quality of processes' in which gender experts engage. (Prügl 2016: 29)

This focus on ethics and quality of process is a key underlying principle for this book, as set out in the final section of this chapter, and explored in more detail in Chapter 5.

It is also useful to consider a practice-focused approach to quality. Drawing on the contributions of both the Gender Manifesto and Madrid Declaration, the Training Centre proposes six key overarching quality criteria for gender training, covering three key aspects of training—quality of content and knowledge; quality of methodologies; and quality of trainers (see Box 1.5).

Box 1.5 UN Women Training Centre overarching quality criteria

- Training for gender equality is part of a feminist political project of transformation of unequal gendered power relations.
- Respect for professional ethics for feminist knowledge transfer.
- Training is embedded training in broader change project and explicitly articulated as part of a Theory of Change.
- Recognition of complexities in practice.
- Adherence to feminist pedagogical principles and practices.
- Intersectional analysis and approach.

Source UN Women Training Centre (2017b).

These aspects of gender training—and the challenges of applying these in practice—are discussed in detail throughout this book. The Training Centre's paper then goes on to propose how such quality criteria can be applied at different stages of the Training Cycle, with the aim of creating *mechanisms* for quality assurance. A number of cross-cutting mechanisms that can be applied across different stages of the Training Cycle are put forward:

- Participatory feasibility assessment and learning needs assessment (Analysis and Planning);
- Theory of Change approach (Analysis and Planning, Evaluation);
- Feminist pedagogical practices (Design and Development, Implementation);
- Feminist/gender-transformative evaluation methods (Design and Development, Evaluation); and
- Peer review and reflexivity (Design and Development, Implementation, Evaluation).

As above with overarching quality criteria, these mechanisms, qualities and skills are discussed throughout the book, in terms of understanding how they can be applied in different training contexts. Figure 1.1 represents the Training Centre's approach to integrating quality criteria and mechanisms at each stage of the Training Cycle. These recommendations offer a useful starting point for collectively defining concrete mechanisms to guide the upholding of quality standards throughout gender training initiatives, taking into consideration the aforementioned focus on ethics and quality of process.

Acknowledging Tensions Over Professionalisation

Processes of professionalisation and establishing quality criteria are not without their challenges. A number of concerns can be highlighted regarding key issues in these processes. For example, as I have asked elsewhere:

> How can we make a claim that someone else's knowledge on gender is wrong – that is, not feminist – and therefore not a true gender approach? Are we saying that only feminists can have gender expertise and knowledge? What, if anything, do we gain for our profession by doing so? (Ferguson 2015: 386)

Following on from this, how can processes of professionalisation and quality criteria deal with gender trainers who do not identify as feminist? What is the role of institutional politics in such a classification? A further point to highlight is the need to reflect on the politics of gender knowledge and how professionalisation processes may serve to further entrench existing hierarchies of knowledge in which well-placed gender trainers become the 'custodians' of gender knowledge (Pialek 2007). Moreover, such notions of superior and hegemonic forms of knowledge "are often associated with Western, Western-professionalized or Western-trained specialists" (Wong et al. 2016: 3), leading to a set of ideas about "a right and a wrong way to 'do' gender in policy contexts" (Standing 2004: 83). As highlighted by the literature on feminist pedagogies—discussed extensively in Chapter 4—the experiences of women of colour have often been marginalised within this field (Kishimoto and Mwangi 2009). Thus, professionalisation and quality processes in gender training should take care not to "deny or silence the contributions of women of colour, particularly when we want to teach students [or training participants] to be critical of the inequalities and hegemonic social structures that are responsible for the world's injustices" (Kishimoto and Mwangi 2009). Therefore, it is important to address assumptions about the identity and location of trainers within intersecting hierarchies—of gender, gender identity, sexuality, class, ethnicity, etc. Insights can be drawn from the field of gender and education here in terms of "teaching about gender inequality from a position of privilege" (Flood 2011), as discussed in more detail in Chapter 5. As such, an intersectional approach to professionalisation and quality is required, in order to embrace ideas around 'teaching vulnerably' and addressing the question of how our own training "affects what we can and cannot see about gender expertise and gender training" (Bustelo et al. 2016a: 172).

In order to tackle some of these challenges, the UN Women Training Centre (2017b) puts forward a number of recommendations for future processes of professionalisation and quality assurance:

- Adopt an intersectional approach;
- Promote the decolonisation of knowledge on gender;
- Pay attention to inequalities already existing within the field of training for gender equality;
- Develop a process that is encouraging and supportive of bringing new actors into the field;

- Focus on peer evaluation as a methodology for reviewing and evaluating quality; and
- Secure funding and human resources to develop and follow up on this process.

These recommendations are positioned as "a first step towards a collective definition, intended to lay a minimum basis for quality criteria and spark debate on how to take forward the development of quality mechanisms" (UN Women Training Centre 2017b: 32). Thus, while no official quality or professionalisation criteria currently exist for gender training, debates around proposed criteria are ongoing. Having set the stage the contemporary dimensions of the field of gender training, the final section now sets out how these issues, tensions and contradictions are explored in the book.

Aims and Approach of the Book

The overall aim of this book is to enhance the potential of gender training as a transformative feminist tool for gender equality, with a focus on advancing both the theory and practice of gender training. First, this book is positioned at a dynamic intersection between theory and practice, drawing equally on the work of researchers and practitioners, as well as those who carefully navigate both fields. The book aims to capitalise on the productive tensions and intellectual and political challenges that arise from such positionalities. This means taking seriously the everyday challenges and frustrations of practitioners working in the field of gender training, while paying attention to the broader structures and patterns identified by feminist academics. These tensions include the tendency for academics to underestimate the complexity of gender training in practice; the difficulties of practitioners engaging in research and writing, particularly when they work on a freelance basis; and the precarity of gender training as a profession, particularly for junior experts. It is worth taking a moment here to reflect on the author's own positionality as a freelance gender specialist, with no fixed income to support the writing of this book. The writing time has been carved out between consultancy projects, all of which have, in turn, enriched the practical experience explored in this book.

Following this, the book adopts a format that aims to be accessible and useful to both academics and practitioners. Where relevant, it includes exercises and examples from practice in order to illustrate key arguments and debates. These are made visible in the book through references to concrete practices and gender trainers/gender training organisations, in order to give credit for the contributions made to the field. While not aiming to serve as a handbook or a manual, this book pairs critical analysis with practical resources and practice-informed case studies that can be used in the practice of gender training. The book relies on a number of key conceptual tools for illustrating the discussions of gender training and grounding these in practice, which are elaborated in more detail throughout the following chapters. Attention is also explicitly paid to the context and type of gender training, to ensure that the examples and issues discussed in this book are as relevant to concrete practical experiences as possible.

In terms of normative and political commitments, the book is guided by an overarching commitment to gender training as a *transformative* tool. This is grounded in an understanding of gender training as both a *feminist* and a *political* endeavour. It means rejecting technocratic and minimalist understandings of gender training, and instead drawing explicitly on feminist pedagogical principles and practices to maximise the space for change within gender training settings and beyond. This explicit focus on transformation sets the book apart from much of the work done by practitioners in the field to date, which focuses on easily applicable tools that are unlikely to generate resistance or contestation. In contrast, this book's approach focuses on how to *harness gender training as a catalyst for disjuncture, rupture and change* in institutions. A second overarching aspect of the analytical approach of the book is an explicit concern with intersectionality and the politics of knowledge. In particular, it responds to the continuing failure of most gender training to integrate intersectionality in a substantive way (Baer et al., n.d.). This means paying attention to *how* knowledge is selected, *which* knowledge is selected, *who delivers* such knowledge through gender training, and *who participates* in gender training. These issues are at the forefront of the analytical and ethical dilemmas explored in the book. In order to acknowledge these very real concerns, the book strives to highlight power dynamics and power relations at all stages of the gender training process—from commissioning, to design, implementation and evaluation. This involves a discussion of the politics of gender training; the role of feminism in the theory and practice of gender training; the challenges of an intersectional practice of gender training; and the unequal power dynamics of gender, class, ethnicity and nationality, among others, that shape the field and all stages of the gender training process.

To explore these issues, the book is developed in the following way. Chapter 2 identifies the key critiques of gender training as a field, and explores how these play out in terms of practical challenges. Next, Chapter 3 explores the relationship between gender training and transformative change, critically reviewing the current academic literature and engaging with work from practice and practice-focused research. A key argument developed throughout the book is that gender training should be guided by feminist pedagogical principles in order to contribute to transformative change projects. Chapter 4 deals specifically with this topic, proposing a core set of principles for the field of gender training—drawing on those put forward by the UN Women Training Centre (2017a)—with a specific focus on how gender trainers can operationalise such principles in gender training processes. The final concluding chapter, Chapter 5, provides a critical overview of the remaining work to be done in the field of gender training, identifying gaps in research and potential future alliances. In particular, this involves pointing to potential innovative methodologies and approaches for moving the field forward, with the overall aim of maximising the transformative potential of gender training.

References

Baer, S., Keim, J., & Nowottnick, L. (n.d.). *Intersectionality in Gender+ Training*. Available at http://ww.quing.eu/files/WHY/baer_keim_nowottnick.pdf.

Bustelo, M., Ferguson, L., & Forest, M. (2016a). Conclusions. In M. Bustelo, L. Ferguson, & M. Forest (Eds.), *The Politics of Feminist Knowledge Transfer: Gender Training and Gender Expertise*. Abingdon and New York: Palgrave Macmillan.

Bustelo, M., Ferguson, L., & Forest, M. (2016b). Introduction. In M. Bustelo, L. Ferguson, & M. Forest (Eds.), *The Politics of Feminist Knowledge Transfer: Gender Training and Gender Expertise*. Abingdon and New York: Palgrave Macmillan.

Bustelo, M., Ferguson, L., & Forest, M. (2016c). *The Politics of Feminist Knowledge Transfer*. Abingdon and New York: Palgrave Macmillan.

Caglar, G., Prügl, E., & Zwingel, S. (Eds.). (2013). *Feminist Strategies in International Governance*. London and New York: Routledge.

European Institute for Gender Equality (EIGE). (2013). *Mapping Gender Training in the European Union and Croatia: Synthesis Report*. Luxembourg: Publications House of the European Union. Available at http://eige.europa.eu/rdc/eige-publications/mapping-gender-training-european-union-and-croatia-synthesis-report.

European Institute for Gender Equality (EIGE). (2014). *Quality Assurance Mechanisms for Gender Training in the European Union: Reflections from the Online Discussion*. Vilnius: European Institute for Gender Equality. Available at http://eige.europa.eu/sites/default/files/documents/MH0113604ENC.PDF.

Ferguson, L. (2015). 'This Is Our Gender Person': The Messy Business of Working as a Gender Expert in International Development. *International Feminist Journal of Politics, 17*(3), 380–397.

Flood, M. 2011. Men as Students and Teachers of Feminist Scholarship. *Men and Masculinities, 14*(2), 135–154. http://www.xyonline.net/sites/default/files/Flood,%20Men%20as%20Students%20and%20Teachers%20of%20Feminist%20Scholarship%202011.pdf.

Gender Manifesto: A Call for Critical Reflection on Gender-Oriented Capacity Building and Consultancy. (2006). Available at http://www.gender.de/mainstreaming/GenderManifesto_engl.pdf.

Hoard, S. (2015). *Gender Expertise in Public Policy: Towards a Theory of Policy Success*. Abingdon and New York: Palgrave Macmillan.

Kantola, J. (2010). *Gender and the European Union*. New York: Palgrave Macmillan.

Kishimoto, K., & Mwangi, M. (2009). Critiquing the Rhetoric of "Safety" in Feminist Pedagogy: Women of Color Offering an Account of Ourselves. *Feminist Teacher, 19*(2), 87–102. Available at https://www.stcloudstate.edu/socialresponsibility/articles/documents/01_Kishimoto_FT_19_2.pdf.

KIT and UN Women Training Centre. (2018). *Professional Development Programme for Gender Trainers*. Available at https://www.kit.nl/gender/training/pdpgt/#home.

Krook, M., & Mackay, F. (Eds.). (2015). *Gender, Politics and Institutions: Towards a Feminist Institutionalism*. Abingdon and New York: Palgrave Macmillan.

Lombardo, E., & Forest, M. (Eds.). (2012). *The Europeanization of Gender Equality Policies: A Discursive-Sociological Approach*. Basingstoke and New York: Palgrave Macmillan.

Mukhopadhyay, M. (2013). Mainstreaming Gender or Reconstituting the Mainstream? Gender Knowledge in Development. *Journal of International Development, 26*(3), 356–367.

Olivius, E., & Rönnblom, M. (2017). 'In the Business of Feminism: Consultants as Sweden's New Gender Equality Workers?'. Paper Presented at *ECPG Conference*, Lausanne, June 2017. https://ecpr.eu/Filestore/PaperProposal/54e45125-8850-4739-8af8-6210c0536cf5.pdf.

OPERA Team. (2011). *OPERA Final Report: Advancing Gender+Training in Theory and Practice*. Prepared by L. Ferguson & M. Forest. QUING: Quality in Gender+Equality Policies. Available at http://www.quing.eu/files/results/final_opera_report.pdf.

Pialek, N. (2007). Gender Mainstreaming in Development Organizations Organizational Discourse and the Perils of Institutional Change. In L. A. Duran, N. D. Payne, A. Duran, & A. R. Garrido (Eds.), *Building Feminist Movements and Organizations: Global Perspectives*. New York: Zed Books.

Prügl, E. (2016). How to Wield Feminist Power. In M. Bustelo, L. Ferguson, & M. Forest (Eds.), *The Politics of Feminist Knowledge Transfer: Gender Training and Gender Expertise*. Abingdon and New York: Palgrave Macmillan.

QUING. (2011, February 3–4). *Madrid Declaration on Advancing Gender+Training in Theory and Practice*. Madrid: Complutense University. Available at http://www.quing.eu/files/madrid_declaration.pdf.

Standing, H. (2004). Gender, Myth and Fable: The Perils of Mainstreaming in Sector Bureaucracies. Repositioning Feminisms in Development. *IDS Bulletin, 35*(4), 82–88.

Thompson, H., & Prügl, E. (2015). *Gender Experts and Gender Expertise: Results of a Survey*. Geneva: Graduate Institute of Geneva. Available at http://graduateinstitute.ch/files/live/sites/iheid/files/sites/genre/shared/Genre_docs/2342_TRavauxEtRecherches/WP_8_2015_Thompson_Pruegl.pdf.

UN Women Training Centre. (2015a, September 16). *Joint Statement from Expert Group Meeting on Training for Gender Equality*. Santo Domingo: UN Women Training Centre. Available at https://trainingcentre.unwomen.org/mod/data/view.php?d=6&rid=389.

UN Women Training Centre. (2015b). *Training for Gender Equality: Twenty Years On*. Santo Domingo: UN Women Training Centre. Available at http://www.unwomen.org/en/digital-library/publications/2015/9/training-for-gender-equality-twenty-years-on.

UN Women Training Centre (2016). *Typology on Training for Gender Equality*. Santo Domingo: UN Women Training Centre. Available at http://www.unwomen.org/en/digital-library/publications/2016/5/typology-on-training-for-gender-equality.

UN Women Training Centre. (2017a). *Working Paper Series: Feminist Pedagogies in Training for Gender Equality*. Prepared by Dr. Lucy Ferguson. Santo Domingo: UN Women Training Centre. Available at https://trainingcentre.unwomen.org/pluginfile.php/72/mod_data/content/40218/02%20Feminist%20Pedagogies%20.pdf.

UN Women Training Centre. (2017b). *Working Paper Series: Quality in Training for Gender Equality*. Prepared by Dr. Lucy Ferguson. Santo Domingo: UN Women Training Centre. Available at https://trainingcentre.unwomen.org/pluginfile.php/72/mod_data/content/40218/03%20Quality%20Assurance.pdf.

UN Women Training Centre. (2018). *Community of Practice (CoP)*. Available at https://trainingcentre.unwomen.org/course/view.php?id=67.

UN Women Training Centre. (n.d.). *About Us*. Available at https://trainingcentre.unwomen.org/mod/page/view.php?id=45&lang=en.

Wenger, E. (1998). Communities of Practice: Learning, Meaning and Identity. *Journal of Mathematics Teacher Education, 6*(2), 185–194.

Wenger, E. (2007). *Communities of Practice and Social Learning Systems: The Career of a Concept*. Available at https://wenger-trayner.com/wp-content/uploads/2012/01/09-10-27-CoPs-and-systems-v2.01.pdf.

Wong, F., Vaast, C., & Mukhopadhyay, M. (2016). *Review and Mapping Exercise for Conceptualizing Professional Development of Gender Trainers: A Working Paper Developed for UN Women Training Centre and KIT*. Santo Domingo and Amsterdam, The Netherlands: UN Women Training Centre and the Royal Tropical Institute (KIT).

CHAPTER 2

Critiques and Challenges in Contemporary Gender Training

Abstract This chapter sets out the key critiques of gender training from the academic literature, such as the claim that gender training has become a 'normalising technology' (Davids and van Eerdewijk in: Bustelo et al. (Eds.) The Politics of Feminist Knowledge Transfer: Gender Training and Gender Expertise, Palgrave Macmillan, Abingdon and New York, 2016, 87) or that debates over gender inequalities are pushed from the realm of politics into the realm of expertise (Kunz in: Bustelo et al. (Eds.) The Politics of Feminist Knowledge Transfer: Gender Training and Gender Expertise, Palgrave Macmillan, Abingdon and New York, 2016). In response to these critiques, the chapter engages substantively with some of the key challenges of gender training from the perspective of reflexive practice, exploring some of the issues that stop gender training contributing to transformative change. The main point highlighted here is the need to work strategically within the constraints of gender training processes and scenarios.

Keywords Co-optation · Neoliberal feminism · Technocracy Intersectionality · Reflexive practice

The contemporary theory and practice of gender training involves a number of key tensions and challenges. These have been raised as matters of debate and concern by practitioners and researchers, and discussed in fora such as the OPERA Conference on Gender+ Training in 2011 (QUING 2011); the Expert Group Meeting on Training for

L. Ferguson, *Gender Training*, Gender and Politics,
https://doi.org/10.1007/978-3-319-91827-3_2

Gender Equality in 2015 (UN Women Training Centre 2015a); and the UN Women Community of Practice (CoP), including a number of Webinars and Virtual Dialogues between 2013 and 2017. Key early works that identified tensions in gender training include the Revisiting Gender Training sourcebook (Mukhopadhyay and Wong 2007) and Standing's work (2004). This chapter explores these key debates in more detail in order to better understand the field, with the overall objective of understanding how gender training can be a transformative tool. In order to do this, the chapter is developed in two substantive sections. The first section deals with major critiques of gender training, and gender expertise in general, which predominantly emerge from the academic literature. Two such strands of critique are identified and explored here. One involves the arguments developed by postcolonial feminists, who posit that practices like gender training are part of the logic of governmentalities. Their analyses are concerned with the politics of knowledge and the power dynamics inherent in gender training and gender expertise. Another related critique emerges from academics who are critical of the so-called neoliberal feminism. The claim here is that gender trainers and experts are complicit in further embedding the logic of neoliberal feminism, in which feminist ideals and politics have been co-opted by the needs of neoliberal institutions.

Following this, three substantive sections address some of the key challenges for contemporary gender training, all of which are discussed in more detail at other points in this book. These emerge primarily from the literature by practitioners, or academic literature developed by researchers grounded in practice. The first issue regards a prevalence of 'technocratic' or 'problem-solving' ways of addressing gender equality, as opposed to more transformative approaches which deal with gender inequalities in highly politicised ways. Another challenge is how to operationalise an intersectional approach to gender training. There is a general agreement across the field that gender training has failed to adequately address the issue of intersectionality. A third issue is that of resistances, which are a necessary—yet difficult—aspect of any gender training process. In this chapter—and throughout the book—I propose that the critiques and challenges identified here are not insurmountable. While it is important to acknowledge these issues and continue to debate them, I suggest that there are causes for optimism in the transformative potential of gender training. This argument is developed more substantively in the concluding section of this chapter.

Critiques of Gender Training

Here I am concerned with *critiques of* gender training, that is, approaches which are either ambivalent or strongly critical about the impact of such practices in terms of their outcomes for gender equality. The majority of these critiques come from authors who are primarily based in academic institutions, rather than those grounded in practice. Nevertheless, many such critiques are based on critical reflections of practice by academics who also practise gender training. It should be acknowledged that these critiques tend to span both gender training *and* gender expertise. As there is little specific literature on gender training and the issues remain salient for both types of work, these are worth expounding here. Two key critiques are outlined in this section—governmentalities/postcolonialism and co-optation. Such critiques—grounded in governmentalities and postcolonial perspectives—are centred on a notion of knowledge transfer processes as inherently political and contested processes which are loaded with power dynamics.

These authors draw on the Foucauldian concept of *governmentalities* and explore "the challenges, dangers, and opportunities of governmentalities in feminist knowledge transfer" (Davids and van Eerdewijk 2016). Caglar et al. (2013: 5) suggest that gender experts produce policy-relevant knowledge, which—in Foucault's words—"induces effects of power." In other words, knowledge makes things governable and constantly draws the boundaries of acceptable behaviour in a specific policy field (Caglar et al. 2013: 5). As Mukhopadhyay (2014) points out, expertise refers to a complex mix of professionals, truth claims and technical procedures that make it possible for authorities—i.e. governments, multilateral institutions, donor bodies and international NGOs—to make their version of gender reality operable. Within this framing, it is posited that gender training has become a 'disciplining mechanism', building new selves that have internalised these mentalities of difference to such an extent that external controls, oversights and incentives are no longer necessary. As Davids and van Eerdewijk (2016: 87) argue, "gender training has become a normalizing technology that has installed itself as a rapidly growing profession." They are also concerned with the ways in which gender experts and trainers have gained voice in these processes, rather than the voices of social movements. Kunz refers to this as "the demobilization of local social movements, a narrowing of feminist political vocabularies, and the marginalization of alternative feminist agendas"

(Kunz 2016: 108). As discussed below, how do feminist gender trainers navigate these claims in order to develop a form of gender training that is able to respond to these kinds of critiques?

A related concern is the postcolonial dimension of the practice of gender training and gender expertise. As Bustelo et al. (2016b: 15) ask, "how can feminist actors address the power relations embedded within the process of feminist knowledge transfer between institutions and actors of the Global North and the Global South?" Kunz's detailed study of gender experts in Liberia engages explicitly with such concerns. She shows how the feminist knowledge transfer scenario "reproduces power hierarchies between different actors and forms of feminist knowledges, and processes of in/exclusions, which render solidarities difficult" (2016: 100). In the Liberia case study, "the authority of knowledge is located with international gender experts or the western feminist knowledge to be transferred, or with local gender experts trained by internationals. This establishes a hierarchy of feminist knowledges and ways of legitimate thinking and acting on WPS [Women, Peace and Security]" (Kunz 2016: 108). Moreover, feminist knowledge tends to be conceptualised as a form of expertise, disavowing gender as a category of critical analytics for disruption and contestation, as discussed below. The consequence of this, Kunz argues, is that the debate regarding gender inequalities is pushed from the realm of politics into the realm of expertise (ibid.). How, then, can gender training be developed in order to allow for 'disruption and contestation'?

The second key critique of gender training and gender expertise is the role of such processes in embedding neoliberal political and economic structures. As Caglar et al. have argued:

> Thus in becoming part of international institutions, feminist strategizing develops its own rationality: to govern through subtle and indirect means. In this context feminist strategizing is turned from a mode of resistance into an instrument of power. (2013: 5–6)

A major concern here is the 'diluting' of feminist theory and politics in the everyday practice of gender expertise and gender training. This means that, in practice, 'gender' has been disassociated from the structural inequalities which form the basis of feminist thought. As a consequence, this "has also made it more acceptable to institutions, since 'doing gender' does not entail addressing structures producing inequalities in general, not only gender inequalities" (Mukhopadhyay 2014: 360). Desai (2007: 801), for example, notes how feminist insights and demands have been "transformed into managerial solutions" that do not address structural inequalities. Mukhopadhyay (2016) argues that gender experts and trainers are governed through a "dominant set of practices and technologies of power" in development. These have, in turn, "structured and shaped" the ways that experts and trainers govern themselves, thus undermining feminist practice. Reflections from the field of international development have shown how gender concerns have often 'evaporated' when translated into practice (Porter and Sweetman 2005), while 'doing gender' is often conflated with, and reduced to, 'helping women' (Cornwall 2007: 73–74). At best, it seems that gender experts have not generated the transformative change hoped of them (Cornwall et al. 2007). For Fraser (2009: 114), this separation between feminism and gender expertise is a consequence of the discourse of gender experts becoming independent of the feminist movement, creating 'a strange shadowy version of itself' or 'an uncanny double'. What is clear is that particular aspects of gender and feminist politics have been included in mainstream agendas, while others have been marginalised and undermined (Prügl and Lustgarten 2006). How, then, can the potential of gender training to contribute to transformative be maximised, and what kinds of theories and methodologies are required to achieve this?

Related to this, a further thematic critique of gender expertise and gender training is the "instrumentalization and co-optation of feminism" (Kunz 2016: 103). Others have argued that contemporary gender initiatives such as microcredit programs represent "a story of co-optation of feminist empowerment rhetorics" (Keating et al. 2010: 172), drawing women further into coercive market relations under the guise of empowerment (ibid.: 156). This maps on to broader critiques of 'neoliberal feminism' (Prügl 2015, 2017; Roberts 2015) and is contextualised within the rise of the "business case for gender equality." This involves presenting gender equality in terms of its benefits for other issues, not as a goal in itself of from a human rights/social justice perspective. Such arguments are now highly familiar to feminists and will not be explored in detail here (see, e.g., Ferguson 2015, for an in-depth review of this approach). In practice, this framework boils down to an approach of "ask not what you can do for gender equality, but what gender equality can do for you." Kothari (2005: 440) places the blame for this on gender professionals themselves, arguing that they (we) "tend to prioritize increasing women's participation in economic processes rather than uncovering and addressing broader unequal power relations between men and women." For Lazreg (2002), gender training represents merely "another link in the chain of the normalization of the development enterprise in the global era through a convergence of academic feminism and organizational interests." What can a feminist notion of gender training contribute to countering these claims, and how can we argue for the value of gender training as a transformative feminist tool?

It is clear that there are strong critiques of the practice of gender training in itself. However, more nuanced versions of these critiques are available from those whose work is grounded in practice. By acknowledging these tensions and exploring how such contradictions play out in practice, such work moves beyond the somewhat fatalistic approach of the critiques outlined above and aims to engage in a more concrete manner with the pragmatic difficulties of gender expertise and gender training on the ground. As such, from an 'outsider' academic perspective, gender experts are merely helping to embed a purely neoliberal version of gender equality, in which our primary goal is to foster the 'rational economic woman' (Rankin 2002). However, this analysis relies on a limited acknowledgement of the constant processes of negotiation and renegotiation in which gender experts engage. As such, the focus of the remainder of the book is on how lessons from practice can enrich our understanding of the potential for gender training to contribute to feminist processes and feminist outcomes.

Practical Challenges: Technocratic vs. Transformative Gender Training

As this chapter has established, the institutional and political contexts of contemporary gender training often demand a *technocratic* form of training, focusing on 'checklists' and 'simple answers' (UN Women Training Centre 2017a). Prügl's (2010) review demonstrates that the majority of gender training manuals exclude any exercise based on reflexivity, and there is a lack of time and space assigned to assessing both trainees' and trainer's positionality. As Mukhopadhyay argues:

> The most common standardized form of training [...] is a short, event-oriented and workshop bounded form presenting 'gender' as a set of skills, which can be straightforwardly delivered and reproduced. (2014: 362)

This is particularly challenging for an approach to gender training which aims to "resist easy answers and disallow the maintenance of homogenous neatness" (Miller 2005: 36), as discussed in more detail in Chapter 4 on feminist pedagogies. As I have discussed elsewhere, a key component of this kind of work is 'getting gender right'—that is, developing messages on gender that will both appeal to institutions and promote change within them. While in academic contexts plenty of time is spent reflecting on the power of knowledge, positionality and epistemology, in practice these debates have to be internalised by gender experts wishing to get a clear message across. It is highly challenging to move from a reflective environment, where knowledge claims are constantly challenged and reformulated, to one in which gender knowledge is demanded in an instant. For example, the World Bank employees in Bedford's study (2007: 296) noted that "it's not that you can do everything, right? Because the Bank is very rigid," while another explained that "the World Bank has an absolutely technocratic vision of gender." This leads to a scenario in which years of reflection are consolidated into certain set messages and arguments. The threat of alienating senior management with 'too much gender' is ever-present. A troubling consequence of such a process in terms of gender training is the 'fixing' of knowledge on gender. Once established, these claims and arguments then become somewhat crystallised and static, despite changes in thinking, research and global socioeconomic developments (Ferguson 2015).

In gender training, this means that the definitions, methods and tools used can often become stagnated. As gender trainers have little space for critical reflection in between trainings—and this is rarely demanded of them (or even discouraged) in any case by commissioning institutions—there is a danger that the 'gender training toolkit' becomes increasingly stripped of its feminist roots and begins to fit more and more neatly into technocratic frameworks. In effect, the demand for gender training to deliver coherent 'answers' and 'solutions' to gender issues robs gender trainers of reflexivity, a key component of feminist research and activism. As gender trainers, we are forced to pin down a single presentation and construction of gender and apply it to the relevant training or institutional context (Ferguson 2015). Mukhopadhyay and Wong (2007) suggest that the emphasis of gender training is "on knowing definitions and replication." This is a pressure widely acknowledged by trainers and experts working in the field of gender equality, often working in contexts where there is a demand for precisely the easy answers and "homogenous neatness"—in the form of 'toolkits' and 'practical skills'—that are antithetical to feminist pedagogical principles, as discussed in more detail in Chapter 4. A concern then is that gender experts, including trainers, "draw their authority not from any political position but from their ability to make feminist knowledge fit into programmes of government" (Milward et al. 2015). This is problematic for gender trainers, who struggle with different ways to explore feminist knowledge in training scenarios, and reflects the critiques of co-optation and instrumentalisation outlined above.

In order to understand the tensions between technocratic and more politicised approaches to gender training, it is useful to explore the role of feminism in gender training. As many practitioners and researchers have argued, in practice there is often strong resistance to the term 'feminist'—from commissioners, trainees and even gender trainers themselves. As noted by Bustelo et al. (2016b: 15–16), this issue was raised several times in the OPERA expert meetings and online fora. One reason identified was that some consider the political goal of transforming gender relations implicit in gender mainstreaming to be 'feminist'—that is, "excessively based on ideological and emotional rather than on rational, scientific, or legal arguments." In response, gender trainers often practise what they call 'calculated ambiguity', in which they may omit the word 'feminist' or 'feminism' explicitly from their training, while at the same time maintaining a commitment to feminist politics and practices. As Chant (2012) argues, there are many scenarios in which there is a need to 'sell' gender to sceptical institutional staff and, in particular, senior management with the power to finance gender activities. In these cases, it is important for gender knowledge to be packaged and presented in a simple yet fundamentally inoffensive way—by developing what Chant calls 'tactical slogans' (2012: 201). However, it should not be taken for granted that all gender trainers and experts are necessarily feminists. As argued elsewhere (Ferguson, 2015), a key challenge for gender training and gender expertise is the prevalence of 'non-feminist work on gender', as discussed in Chapter 1. Specifically:

> If nonfeminist or even antifeminist people are working on gender, this creates a great deal of work for us to 'undo'. In such situations, it becomes much harder to negotiate feminist key messages and get these established within an institution or policy area. It also becomes necessary to argue against the already established wisdom on gender that has been developed by non-gender experts or nonfeminists. (Ferguson 2015: 386)

This raises questions about the value of 'hiding feminism' versus being explicit and open about the politics of gender training processes. As argued throughout this book, if gender training is to be a transformative tool, it needs to be embedded in a highly political and contested process of change in gendered power dynamics and relations.

In order to deal with these challenges, gender trainers and gender experts enact pragmatic strategies to maximise the transformative potential of their work. Such processes are not 'one-way', but rather involve a process of negotiation between gender trainers and training commissioners over what 'gender' does and does not mean in each specific training context (as discussed in more detail in Chapter 4). As Eyben (2007: 65) notes: "I describe dreary, bureaucratic arguments over the choice of words and pictures as 'battles' because that is how I experienced them." That is, by drawing on real-life conversations, 'battles', confrontations and negotiations, we are able to bring into sharp focus the political nature of gender training and explore this in a more substantive way. A number of detailed studies on the work of gender experts exist, such as Campbell and Teghtsoonian's (2010) analysis of gender experts in Kyrgyzstan. Their research presents a shrewd analysis of how gender experts change their expectations and objectives over time, acknowledging the limitations of this work: "(G)ender advocates can only hope that getting the texts right – aligning the language and inserting appropriate indicators, for example – will have practical benefits for women on the ground" (ibid.: 191).

Box 2.1: Example of a conversation between gender trainers and commissioners

Reflecting on my work within a particular UN agency, I can still recall a number of conversations in which I have been called to 'show how this will benefit the sector', to 'take out the gender bit', and in which it has been made clear that if we 'don't highlight the benefits of doing this, we will not get any support'. Of particular concern is the stripping down of empowerment to its economic—that is, income-generating—components. I have been asked to 'take out the social and political empowerment bit and just focus on the economic side' or to 'take out the human rights and equality bit'. Some areas, it seems, are particularly out of bounds. I have struggled specifically with the issue of social reproduction, on which I have also conducted research. Even framing this issue in the most accessible and non-confrontational ways possible—as the importance of childcare provision and parental rights—meets a wall of resistance: 'you'll have to take that bit out; they won't want to hear about that'. The moments after such conversations involve a challenging time of political and personal reflection, sometimes even a bit of crying in the toilets. These are the spaces in which the possibilities for feminist influence seem to close down around us. As my key research findings centre on the impact of a specific sector on social reproduction, it is highly frustrating to have to remove this issue from reports and presentations in which I have been asked to present as an expert by institutions concerned with this sector.

Source Author's own elaboration based on first-hand research, including interviews with gender trainers.

As such, gender trainers find creative ways to negotiate and push back against the technocratic and bureaucratising urges of institutions. These involve crafting out political space for discussions and debates, and working along feminist pedagogical lines, as discussed extensively in Chapter 4.

Practical Challenges: Integrating Intersectionality

A concern with intersectionality is an overarching aspect of the analytical approach of this book, as highlighted in Chapter 1. As noted extensively in the literature on the application of intersectional feminist theory to gender equality policies, the "quality of engagement of the equality architecture with intersectionality" varies across institutional and policy contexts (Walby et al. 2012: 434; Enderstein 2017). Hancock (2007) outlines three key approaches to intersectionality in equality policy: 'unitary', in which each inequality is treated separately; 'multiple', where categories of inequality are all considered equally important in a predetermined relation with each other; and 'intersectional', wherein categories are all equally important but their relation to one another remains an empirically open question. Extensive analysis of intersectional gender equality policies in the European Union (EU) concludes that the most common approach followed by the EU and many of its member states has been one closer to a 'multiple', rather than an 'intersectional', approach (Kantola and Nousiainen 2009; Lombardo and Verloo 2009). As Bustelo et al. argue (2016b: 17):

> This European approach, which is also similar to the approaches of many international organizations, has influenced much of the gender training and gender expertise propagated by European governments and international organizations, thus substantially limiting the development of a truly intersectional approach.

In addition to—or perhaps because of—the narrow vision of intersectionality theory to gender equality policies, the application of an intersectional approach in the practice of gender training has, to date, remained limited. Currently, "intersectionality is not fully integrated in regular gender training experiences in any explicit way" (Bustelo et al. 2016a: 167). In order for this to change, intersectionality must be explicitly addressed both theoretically—i.e. within training content—and practically—i.e. in the methods employed by training—and included in all aspects of the training (Wong et al. 2016).

While intersectionality may not be *institutionalised* in any substantive way in gender training, there are nevertheless a number of promising examples from practice which point to how this may be improved. For example, while the authors in Bustelo et al. (2016a: 168) edited collection on gender training and gender expertise do not explicitly integrate intersectionality in their trainings,

> Most authors do reflect on the ways in which intersectionality influences how power dynamics play out in knowledge transfer scenarios. That is, while this may not be explicitly integrated into the content of a training course, for example, practitioners and researchers nevertheless reflect on the intersectional power dynamics of a training scenario, and how this produces hierarchies of knowledge in different contexts. As such, this suggests that intersectionality is always present in any knowledge transfer scenario, just as gender is always necessarily one hierarchy among many in any context. Moreover, the situated knowledges on gender drawn upon in such scenarios are embedded in intersectional power dynamics. Therefore, we suggest that the different authors find feminist ways of bringing intersectionality on board in training and expertise scenarios, whether this is done in an explicit or implicit manner.

A recent study by Enderstein (2018) sheds some light on the intersectional practice of gender trainers and is worth discussing here at some length. In order to explore the "micro-level dynamics of the practice of gender trainers," Enderstein conducted in-depth semi-structured interviews with 15 participants working as gender trainers in the EU. Her First, the trainers interviewed highlighted a lack of support from training commissioners for including intersectionality in the content of gender trainings. This was compounded by a lack of acknowledgement of the historical embeddedness of intersectionality on the part of institutions. Drawing on the challenges posed by technocratic approaches to gender training outlined above, a similar trend can be identified with an overtly feminist or political approach to intersectionality. As Enderstein argues, "a checkbox application of intersectionality is antithetical to the history of the concept itself, in order to preserve the political and transformative capacity of intersectionality we need to be aware of its genealogy and origins." One interviewee, Eleni, suggests that "most people just want it like a fancy word [...] also to tick the box of feeling good about ourselves and our organisations." Findings demonstrate a number of innovative ways in which gender trainers approach intersectionality in their work, both as an analytical paradigm and as a practical tool. In order to combat this, Eleni explicitly draws on the 'historical present' in her trainings, making reference to the socio-political history of the training context.

A second finding concerns the practical ways in which intersectional thinking is integrated into gender training scenarios. Enderstein's interviewees shared a strong commitment to responding to what groups of participants bring to the training scenario, as opposed to relying on identity categories as straightforward indications of how the session will unfold. One trainer, Julia, discusses a form of *responsiveness* as a way of working with intersectionality. This involves "close attention to the composition and interaction of the group itself and the understanding that it is necessary to respond to emergent categories of difference specific to the time and space of the training scenario" (Enderstein 2018). While the design of gender training may be based on predetermined categories of differences, in their practical interactions gender trainers are able to apply an approach to intersectionality that "relies on emergent and situated identity categories which are linked to a specific time and place" (ibid.). In the case of intersectionality, this involves confronting power and privilege and requires trainers to facilitate 'learning through difference' (ibid.).

Related to this, the trainers interviewed highlighted the importance of an 'affective connection' for working with intersectionality in tandem with workshop participants. This is also a fundamental component of feminist pedagogies for gender training, which are discussed more substantively in Chapter 4.

Finally, Enderstein's (2018: 15) study highlights the importance of the gender trainer as an intersectional subject. She describes this as "another intersectional subjectivity at play within gender training scenarios which is often unacknowledged." Again, this draws on key aspects of feminist pedagogical principles and practices as explored in Chapter 4. Gender trainers are able to draw on their own histories and identities in order to address resistances, and to ground themselves explicitly in an application of intersectionality to the training scenario of which they are also a part, rather than somehow 'outside' of. This requires "self-reflection and learning journeys" (ibid.) by gender trainers, part of a broader approach which involves a "reciprocal and temporally progressive evolution over time, for both gender trainers and workshop participants" (ibid.: 18). This speaks to the issue of positionality, discussed in Chapter 1, and the importance of reflexivity as a key principle in gender training, as noted in Chapter 4.

Practical Challenges: Resistances

The third practical challenge addressed here is resistances to gender training. Resistances are a fundamental part of transformative gender training and can be understood as productive tensions that are required in order to move forward with a process of personal and institutional change towards gender equality. This issue is discussed in more detail in Chapter 3—in an exploration of *institutional resistances*—while here I focus more specifically on different kinds of *individual resistances* to gender training. Lombardo and Mergaert's (2016) work is particularly useful here. They categorise individual resistances at a number of different levels and in different forms—implicit, explicit, gender specific or not gender specific. They demonstrate that resistance from training participants tends to be similar across a wide range of training contexts. Three main forms of individual resistance are identified by Lombardo and Mergaert (2016)—"denial of the need for gender change," "trivialising gender equality" and "refusing to accept responsibility for solving the problem." With regard to the first, for example, training participants are often resistant to the very idea of gender equality as a legitimate goal, which Lombardo and Mergaert refer to as the 'mirage of equality'. Research on gender training in the private sector, for instance, shows that many people regard gender equality as an issue that is 'out of fashion' and which can, therefore, be 'skipped' (Ferguson and Moreno 2016: 69). Their perception is that "women and men are equally situated in employment, social life, and so a gender equality debate is useless" (Lombardo and Mergaert 2016: 50). The "denial of the need for gender change" refers to a rejection of the existence of gender inequality, or the belief that gender roles are natural.

Other forms of resistance include trivialising the issue, either by suggesting that gender training is a 'waste of time' or, conversely, trainees who already believe they know everything about gender equality. These participants are referred to by one trainer as "'cool men', who, when a trainer starts to talk about gender equality, frequently comment that they 'already do the washing up'" (Lombardo 2009). An example of refusing to accept responsibility for gender inequality is embedded in a broader tension—as identified above and in Chapter 3—that gender inequality is seen as a problem of 'others', and does not apply to Western European countries or the internal dynamics of international and development agencies. As Lombardo and Mergaert argue, these kinds of arguments serve to "legitimize the claim that a change in gender norms is unnecessary" (Lombardo and Mergaert 2016: 53). These kinds of resistances can be linked to the discussions of privileges—in particular the ways in which certain kinds of privilege are invisible to training participants—as discussed in more detail in Chapter 5.

While it is useful to categorise these different kinds of individual resistances, caution should be taken in making assumptions about training participants based on their behaviour in training scenarios. As Verloo and the QUING Consortium (2012) argue, gender issues tend to be seen as personal issues by training participants, and as such gender training can be seen as intrusive. As gender training challenges participants' identity and beliefs, participants may interpret this as a form of attack (Lombardo and Mergaert 2013). This highlights the importance of engaging feminist pedagogical principles in gender training, as discussed in more detail in Chapter 4. In addition, individual resistances need to be placed in the specific institutional context in which they take place, as elaborated in Chapter 3.

A further issue—as highlighted by Kunz (2016: 107)—is the ways in which gender training can "contribute to discursive mechanisms of in/exclusion which marginalize particular identities." She cites the 'wo/man troublemaker', who questions the implementation of gender mainstreaming or gender equality legislation (in this particular case, UN Security Council Resolution 1325). Kunz's concern is that those who do not fall into line with the feminist knowledge transfer process may reflect racialised stereotypes of the 'angry brown woman', who is not taken seriously and sidelined or disciplined (cited from Razack 2004). As Kunz (2016: 108) argues, "this scenario of feminist knowledge transfer marginalizes subjects who resist or subvert the process, or who choose to engage on their own terms, or not to engage at all." This calls, then, for a more subtle reading of resistances—one which engages with the personal experiences and identities of participants, and allows space for participants to contest, disrupt and reject a one-way understanding of a knowledge transfer process.

In addition to these academic reflections on resistances, useful contributions can be drawn from more informal literature. For example, in 2015, the UN Women Training Centre (2015b) conducted a Webinar and Virtual Dialogue on Resistances. A number of insightful discussions emerged from this process, as highlighted in the box below.

Box 2.2: Key points on resistances raised by the UN Women Training Centre's 2015 Virtual Dialogue

- Webinar panellist Elisabeth Prügl argued that resistance to gender training results from the fact that such training is highly political, and that treating gender training as a form of democratic politics may help to deal with resistances.
- Panellist Lut Mergaert highlighted that it is always useful to understand *what* people are resisting when they manifest resistances in gender training.
- Panellist Maitrayee Mukhodopadhyay reiterated that gender training is not just about *the mechanics of doing gender*, but rather the *politics of doing gender* and the understanding of social relations—a highly useful distinction which relates to the discussion regarding technocratic gender training above. She also identified four main sources from which resistance arise:

- Differing meanings of gender and gender equality, e.g. equality as sameness; affirming difference from the male norm and equality as transforming all established gender norms.
- Epistemological differences. Gender equality is especially challenging in institutions whose core business is scientific or technical. Resistances concern how evidence of gender equality is constructed and how relevant this is to the core business of the institution.
- Opposing the power of global discourses. Resistance is manifest by developing country bureaucrats who face increasing conditions from donors and international agencies. This also entails resistance against a universal ideal, which is difficult to translate across contexts.
- The gendered self. As we are all gendered and have opinions about gender, this is a source of tension when training programmes lack the time to explore individual understandings.

Source UN Women Training Centre (2015b) *Virtual Dialogue on Resistances in Training for Gender Equality.*

Box 2.3: Ways of addressing resistances proposed by the UN Women Training Centre's 2015 Virtual Dialogue

Collectively, a number of strategies or tools to support gender trainers in dealing with resistance were proposed during the UN Women Training Centre's 2015 Webinar and Virtual Dialogue forum discussion on resistances:

- Provide clear facts, figures and examples, which are as close as possible to the participants' realities. The trainer must draw on his/her own knowledge.
- Listen carefully to participants' objections and ask questions to ascertain where the problem lies. When institutional or process-related elements like a lack of resources are at play, participants could be invited to find solutions together in group discussions.

- Make resistances visible and investigate their causes so as to find solutions.
- Focus on the core business of the institution commissioning the training and ensure that trainers are knowledgeable about the sector they are dealing with.
- Spend time on gender analysis rather than solely on tools and procedures to mainstream gender.
- Allow for debate on gender concepts, even in short training sessions. For example, one way to address gender subjectivity is to hold structured feedback sessions and ask resistant participants to lead discussions.
- Resistances to gender training can often be born from fear—fear of losing power and privileges, of uncertainties, of painful truth, of upsetting the status quo and of self-examination. As such, dealing with resistances requires sincerity and honesty about losing power and privileges on the part of both trainers and participants.
- Ensure that resistances are dealt with in a way that involves empathy and compassion for training participants.

Examples of specific techniques were put forth by Webinar panellist Lut Mergaert:

> A technique we use is to ask participants how they believe their colleagues will react when they say they have attended gender training and explain what they have learnt. They anticipate potential reactions and work out how to respond. A debate occurs automatically as they start mixing expected reactions from colleagues with their own preconceptions about the concepts addressed.

Further examples were also highlighted by Webinar panellist Maitrayee Mukhodopadhyay:

> There is a real urgency to go beyond technical aspects. This is not just about what gender means overall, but about asking participants what gender equality means to them. My most recent training experience was with high-level bureaucrats in Kurdistan, Iraq. We had an hour-long debate on whether gender equality was important for their 5-year plan. This made things more political because issues like what equality meant vis-à-vis the

plan came up. I was willing to sacrifice time that would have gone into getting the 'correct' version of gender equality, or technical issues, across. It was more important that trainees convinced themselves that the plan will work given their own version of gender equality. We have to allow that debate. The politics of gender must be discussed.

Source UN Women Training Centre (2015b) *Virtual Dialogue on Resistances in Training for Gender Equality*.

As discussed in more detail in Chapter 3, resistances to gender training and gender equality present opportunities for gender training to contribute to broader change processes. As Bustelo, Ferguson and Forest (2016a: 170) point out, feminist knowledge transfer requires an "explicit engagement with the very status of resistances in the process of feminist knowledge transfer" as "resistance and contestation must be present in order for such a scenario to be considered 'feminist' and 'transformative'." As such, on the one hand, gender trainers need to develop tools and strategies for addressing resistances in—and to—the training scenario. At the same time, it is important to remember that resistances are a vital part of transformative gender training. The concluding section of this chapter explores how to overcome some of the key critiques and challenges faced by contemporary gender training.

Conclusions

This chapter has highlighted both critiques of and practical challenges to gender training. In terms of the critiques, these present a somewhat pessimistic picture of the potential of gender training as a transformative tool for gender equality. As I have suggested elsewhere (Ferguson 2015: 393), "in the worst case scenario, we are merely contributing to the construction of a legitimized feminist agenda within an increasingly neoliberal and corporate model of development" or "tinkering around with the tool-kit" (Kothari 2005: 444). Moreover, as set out above, for many this is also a practice of postcolonial politics. In order to address this conundrum, Kunz (2016: 109), for example, proposes a number of strategies for opening up "space for decolonizing the circulation of feminist knowledges." She suggests building on Jauhola's notion of the "queered gender advisor, who instead of 'knowing gender' would have the task of interrupting the processes of knowing and subverting the normalised understandings of gender" (Jauhola 2013: 174). This feeds into the overarching arguments developed in this chapter about the importance of contestation in gender training processes. In terms of gender training, this requires "resisting the colonial urge to 'change the other', as well as a critical (self-)reflection on the position of advisors and researchers [and trainers]" (Kunz 2016: 110).

Following on from this, Kunz (2016: 111) also calls for an acknowledgement that "feminist knowledges circulate in many different ways and directions, defying the simplistic, linear top-down version of the transfer scenario." This is a key point for gender training and follows the argument developed here—that gender training is both a political act and a political process, and should explicitly engage with the power dynamics of the training context and broader change processes. It is important to acknowledge the potential for co-optation, neoliberal feminism and postcolonial practices involved in gender training. However, it is only when we engage with the practical challenges of gender training processes and scenarios—as set out in this chapter—that we can better understand the power dynamics involved. By exploring the "specific processes through which transformative impulses are translated into integrative practices" (Campbell and Teghtsoonian 2010: 181), we are better able to seek collective solutions and strategies for addressing these challenges.

This also requires a critical and reflexive practice on the part of gender trainers, in order to ensure an ongoing questioning of the power dynamics in which gender training is embedded, including the specific dynamics of each individual training scenario. As gender trainers, we can embrace the "messiness and ambiguities of our role" and seek "creative and flexible ways of working in order to identify the spaces for potential influence and transformation" (Ferguson 2015: 394), as explored in more detail in Chapters 4 and 5. Overall, this book develops an argument that despite the substantive critiques and challenges, gender training can be a transformative tool for gender equality. The next chapter explores the relationship between gender training and transformative change, in order to establish to what extent such a claim can be made, and what more needs to be done to enhance the transformative potential of gender training.

References

Bedford, K. (2007). The Imperative of Male Inclusion: How Institutional Context Influences World Bank Gender Policy. *International Feminist Journal of Politics, 9*(3), 289–311.

Bustelo, M., Ferguson, L., & Forest, M. (2016a). Conclusions. In M. Bustelo, L. Ferguson, & M. Forest (Eds.), *The Politics of Feminist Knowledge Transfer: Gender Training and Gender Expertise*. Abingdon and New York: Palgrave Macmillan.

Bustelo, M., Ferguson, L., & Forest, M. (2016b). Introduction. In M. Bustelo, L. Ferguson, & M. Forest (Eds.), *The Politics of Feminist Knowledge Transfer: Gender Training and Gender Expertise*. Abingdon and New York: Palgrave Macmillan.

Caglar, G., Prügl, E., & Zwingel, S. (Eds.). (2013). *Feminist Strategies in International Governance*. London and New York: Routledge.

Campbell, M. L., & Teghtsoonian, K. (2010). Aid Effectiveness and Women's Empowerment: Practices of Governance in the Funding of International Development. *Signs, 36*(1), 177–201.

Chant, S. (2012). The Disappearing of 'Smart Economics'? The *World Development Report 2012* on Gender Equality: Some Concerns About the Preparatory Process and the Prospects for Paradigm Change. *Global Social Policy, 12*(2), 198–218.

Cornwall, A. (2007). Revisiting the 'Gender Agenda'. *IDS Bulletin, 38*(2), 69–78.

Cornwall, A., Harrison, E., & Whitehead, A. (Eds.). (2007). *Feminisms in Development: Contradictions, Contestations and Challenges*. London: Zed Books.

Davids, T., & van Eerdewijk, A. (2016). The Smothering of Feminist Knowledge: Gender Mainstreaming Articulated Through Neoliberal Governmentalities. In M. Bustelo, L. Ferguson, & M. Forest (Eds.), *The Politics of Feminist Knowledge Transfer: Gender Training and Gender Expertise* (pp. 80–98). Abingdon and New York: Palgrave Macmillan.

Desai, M. (2007). The Messy Relationship Between Feminisms and Globalizations. *Gender and Society, 21*(6), 797–803.

Enderstein, A. M. (2017). *Working with Intersectionality: Opportunities and Challenges for Gender+Training*. Paper Presented at *ECPG Conference*, Lausanne, June 2016.

Enderstein, A. M. (2018). 'First of All, Gender Is Power': Intersectionality as Praxis in Gender Training. *Studies on Home and Community Science, 11*(2), 44–56.

Eyben, R. (2007). Battles Over Booklets: Gender Myths in the British Aid Programme. In A. Cornwall, E. Harrison, & A. Whitehead (Eds.), *Feminisms in Development: Contradictions, Contestations and Challenges* (pp. 65–78). London: Zed Books.

Ferguson, L. (2015). 'This Is Our Gender Person': The Messy Business of Working as a Gender Expert in International Development. *International Feminist Journal of Politics.* https://doi.org/10.1080/14616742.2014.918787.

Ferguson, L., & Moreno, D. (2016). Gender Expertise and the Private Sector: Navigating the Privatization of Gender Equality Funding. In M. Bustelo, L. Ferguson, & M. Forest (Eds.), *The Politics of Feminist Knowledge Transfer: Gender Training and Gender Expertise* (pp. 62–79). Abingdon and New York: Palgrave Macmillan.

Fraser, N. (2009). Feminism, Capitalism and the Cunning of History. *New Left Review, 56,* 97–117.

Hancock, A. M. (2007). When Multiplication Doesn't Equal Quick Addition: Examining Intersectionality as a Research Paradigm. *Indian Journal of Gender Studies, 19*(2), 63–79.

Jauhola, M. (2013). *Post-tsunami Reconstruction in Indonesia: Negotiating Normativity Through Gender Mainstreaming Initiatives in Aceh.* Abingdon and New York: Routledge.

Kantola, J., & Nousiainen, K. (2009). Institutionalizing Intersectionality in Europe. *International Feminist Journal of Politics, 11*(4), 459–477.

Keating, C., Rasmussen, C., & Rishi, P. (2010). The Rationality of Empowerment: Microcredit, Accumulation by Dispossession, and the Gendered Economy. *Signs, 36*(1), 153–176.

Kothari, U. (2005). Authority and Expertise: The Professionalisation of International Development and the Ordering of Dissent. *Antipode, 37*(3), 425–446.

Kunz, R. (2016). Windows of Opportunity, Trojan Horses, and Waves of Women on the Move: De-colonizing the Circulation of Feminist Knowledges Through Metaphors? In M. Bustelo, L. Ferguson, & M. Forest (Eds.), *The Politics of Feminist Knowledge Transfer: Gender Training and Gender Expertise* (pp. 99–117). Abingdon and New York: Palgrave Macmillan.

Lazreg, D. (2002). Development: Feminist Theory's Cul-de-sac. In K. Saunders (Ed.), *Feminist Post-development Thought: Rethinking Modernity, Postcolonialism and Representation.* London: Zed Books.

Lombardo, E. (Ed.). (2009). *Final TARGET Report for a Policy Oriented Atlantic Project.* Brussels: EACEA.

Lombardo, E., & Mergaert, L. (2013). Gender Mainstreaming and Resistance to Gender Training: A Framework for Studying Implementation. *Journal of Feminist and Gender Research, 21,* 296–311.

Lombardo, E., & Mergaert, L. (2016). Resistance in Gender Training and Mainstreaming Processes. In M. Bustelo, L. Ferguson, & M. Forest (Eds.), *The Politics of Feminist Knowledge Transfer: Gender Training and Gender Expertise* (pp. 43–61). Abingdon and New York: Palgrave Macmillan.

Lombardo, E., & Verloo, M. (2009). Stretching Gender Equality to Other Inequalities: Political Intersectionality in European Gender Equality Policies. In M. Verloo, E. Lombardo, & P. Meier (Eds.), *The Discursive Politics of Gender Equality: Stretching, Bending and Policy-Making*. London: Routledge.

Miller, A. S. (2005). Feminist Pedagogies: Implications of a Liberative Praxis. In K. O. Wicker, A. S. Miller, & M. W. Dube (Eds.), *Feminism New Testament Studies: Global and Future Perspectives*. New York: Routledge.

Milward, K., Mukhopadhyay, M., & Wong, F. (2015). Gender Mainstreaming Critiques: Signposts or Dead Ends? *IDS Bulletin, 46*(4), 75–81.

Mukhopadhyay, M. (2014). Mainstreaming Gender or Reconstituting the Mainstream? Gender Knowledge in Development. *Journal of International Development, 26*, 356–367.

Mukhopaghyay, M. (2016). Introduction. In M. Mukhopaghyay (Ed.), *Feminist Subversion and Complicity: Governmentalities and Gender Knowledge in South Asia*. New Delhi: Zubaan Books.

Mukhopadhyay, M., & Wong, F. (2007) Introduction: Revisiting Gender Training. The Making and Remaking of Gender Knowledge. In M. Mukhopadhyay & F. Wong (Eds.) *Revisiting Gender Training: The Making and Remaking of Gender Knowledge. A Global Sourcebook*. Amsterdam, The Netherlands : The Royal Tropical Institute (KIT).

Porter, F., & Sweetman, C. (2005). Editorial. *Gender and Development, 13*(2), 2–10.

Prügl, E. (2010, October 6–8). *Gender Expertise and Feminist Knowledge*. Presented at the Conference on "Gender Politics in International Governance", Graduate Institute, Geneva.

Prügl, E. (2015). Neoliberalising Feminism. *New Political Economy, 20*(4), 614–631.

Prügl, E. (2017). Neoliberalism with a Feminist Face: Crafting a New Hegemony at the World Bank. *Feminist Economics, 23*(1), 30–53.

Prügl, E., & Lustgarten, A. (2006). Mainstreaming Gender in International Organizations. In J. S. Jaquette & G. Summerfield (Eds.), *Women and Gender Equity in Development Theory and Practice: Institutions, Resources and Mobilization* (pp. 53–70). Durham, NC: Duke University Press.

QUING. (2011). *Madrid Declaration on Advancing Gender+ Training in Theory and Practice*. Complutense University, Madrid, February 3–4. Available at: http://www.quing.eu/files/madrid_declaration.pdf.

Rankin, K. N. (2002). Social Capital, Microfinance, and the Politics of Development. *Feminist Economics, 8*(1), 1–24.

Roberts, A. (2015). The Political Economy of 'Transnational Business Feminism'. *International Feminist Journal of Politics, 17*(2), 209–231.

Standing, H. (2004). Gender, Myth and Fable: The Perils of Mainstreaming in Sector Bureaucracies. *IDS Bulletin: Repositioning Feminisms in Development, 35*(4), 82–88.

UN Women Training Centre. (2015a, September 16). *Joint Statement from Expert Group Meeting on Training for Gender Equality*. Santo Domingo: UN Women Training Centre. Available at: https://trainingcentre.unwomen.org/mod/data/view.php?d=6&rid=389.

UN Women Training Centre. (2015b, May 6–13). *Virtual Dialogue on Resistances in Training for Gender Equality*. Available at: https://trainingcentre.unwomen.org/mod/page/view.php?id=2119.

UN Women Training Centre. (2017). *Working Paper Series: Feminist Pedagogies in Training for Gender Equality*. Prepared by Dr. Lucy Ferguson. Santo Domingo: UN Women Training Centre. Available at: https://trainingcentre.unwomen.org/pluginfile.php/72/mod_data/content/40218/02%20Feminist%20Pedagogies%20.pdf.

Verloo, M., & QUING Consortium. (2012). *Final QUING Report*. Vienna: Institute for Human Sciences.

Walby, S., Armstrong, J., & Strid, S. (2012). Intersectionality: Multiple Inequalities in Social Theory. *Sociology, 46*(2), 224–240.

Wong, F., Vaast, C., & Mukhopadhyay, M. (2016). *Review and Mapping Paper: Conceptualizing Professional Development of Gender Trainers*. Santo Domingo and Amsterdam, The Netherlands: UN Women Training Centre and Royal Tropical Institute (KIT).

CHAPTER 3

Gender Training and Transformative Change

Abstract In this chapter, the possibilities and limitations of gender training for contributing to transformative change for gender equality are explored in detail. The chapter argues for a move beyond a focus on individual change—as demonstrated in current approaches to the evaluation of gender training—and rather on exploring institutional resistances and institutional change. This draws on both academic literature on feminist institutionalism and reflections from practice, with a focus on maximising the impact of gender training on institutional change. A key concern for future work in gender training is the lack of a clearly articulated theory of the relationship between gender training and transformative change. The chapter argues that even without perfect conditions gender trainers can work to maximise the spaces for feminist change within existing constraints and conditions.

Keywords Individual change · Feminist institutionalism Institutional change · Theory of change · Gender-transformative evaluation

An analysis of change is fundamental to gender training, in order to understand *what* contribution it can make to transformative change and *how* such change can be maximised for gender equality. If the ultimate goal of gender training is feminist transformation, what is needed in order for this to be achieved? This chapter explores different approaches to change through gender equality in order to develop a clearer picture

L. Ferguson, *Gender Training*, Gender and Politics,
https://doi.org/10.1007/978-3-319-91827-3_3

of how training contributes to longer-term transformation or change projects. As argued in the UN Women Training Centre's *Theory of Change* paper:

> It is important to note that training by itself cannot bring change. In order for training to be able to contribute to change, it must be embedded in a broader set of measures and actions to influence change, and should be part of a long-term continuous process. (UN Women Training Centre 2017b: 4)

As argued in the Training Centre's *Compendium of Good Practices in Training for Gender Equality*, the extent to which training is embedded in long-term change projects substantively affects the outcomes and impact of training. For example, "participants must feel that there is space to implement what they are learning during a training in their institutional settings" (UN Women Training Centre 2016: 17). Moreover, as highlighted by Mukhopadhyay and Wong (2007: 13), training should be seen as "one of a number of key gender strategies but insufficient by itself." To date, we lack arguments—and evidence—for demonstrating *how*, *for whom*, *why* and *when* training contributes to change in gendered power relations (Bustelo et al. 2016). As Mergaert notes,

> Impact comes not in the short-term, but in the longer-term. [...] it's not with a one-off initiative that you will change a situation, there has to be a coherent approach [at a higher level]. Then the training will contribute something that makes sense. Because if there is no strategy in place and if the institutional preconditions are not fulfilled [...] then the training will not make a difference. (Lut Mergaert, quoted in UN Women Training Centre 2016: 18)

However, it is also important to acknowledge the challenges and failures of these broader change processes—in particular gender mainstreaming. As noted throughout the literature on gender mainstreaming and in the critiques outlined in Chapter 2, the results of such interventions have been ambiguous and often contradictory to the original feminist goals.

Key insights from research on gender mainstreaming demonstrate that gender mainstreaming strategies have lacked a full articulation of a Theory of Change (Daly 2005). Moreover, the Theory of Change underlying many gender mainstreaming actions and strategies is often outdated; based on assumptions that are no longer valid in the contemporary complex economic and political reality; and too narrow or limited, or too short term and pragmatic, forgetting the longer-term social transformations that would lead to sustainable shifts in gender and social power relations (Batliwala 2012). As Eyben et al. (2008: 201) argue, many of the implicit theories of change which underpin gender mainstreaming "may have become so embedded that we no longer question whether they are the most useful for our purpose, or if we are using them as well as we could." In addition, there are currently no substantive methodologies for measuring the impact of gender training (UN Women Training Centre 2015a). Moreover, "there is little systematic assessment of the relationship between organizational change and training for gender equality" and a stark lack of evaluation evidence on gender training. As outlined in UN Women Training Centre's (2018) *Evaluation Tool*: "While there are a variety of publications on the evaluations from a gender perspective of larger programmes and projects, there is very little found specifically on gender training. Some training manuals, especially when designed to be ready-to-use products, contain a small section or short note for the facilitator to distribute an evaluation survey at the end of the workshop, seminar or course." Following on from the discussion of individual resistances in Chapter 2, there is also a pressing need to engage with *institutional* resistances. That is, how do institutions resist and tame feminist ambitions, and does gender training interact with these processes of resistance?

The chapter is developed in three substantive sections. The first explores institutional resistances to change, in the context of both gender training and gender mainstreaming. Following this, the second section engages with academic critiques and analyses of feminist change in institutions, drawing on the literature on feminist institutionalism and gender mainstreaming. In line with the format of the other chapters in this book, the third section looks more to the literature emerging out of the practice of gender expertise, and gender training in particular—exploring Theory of Change approaches and evaluation. I argue that such approaches need to be developed more substantively in order to set more realistic expectations about the impact of gender training processes, and understand more clearly the ways in which gender training contributes to—or does not contribute to—change. The concluding section of the chapter offers some reflections on the ways in which gender training can contribute to transformative change, and what kinds of strategies might be employed for maximising the impact of such change.

Institutional Resistances

As explored in Chapter 2, a range of individual resistances to gender training can be identified—explicit versus implicit, gender specific versus non-gender specific, etc. Here, the focus is on understanding resistances from an institutional perspective—that is, what are the specific ways in which gender training is blocked from contributing to transformative change through its engagement with institutions? As argued by Davids and Van Eerdewijk (2016: 87), "the demand for gender expertise has been accompanied by the decay of gender infrastructure." Thus, gender mainstreaming interventions are caught in a contradictory dynamic in which, on the one hand, there is increasing demand for and reliance on experts and expertise, while, on the other hand, internal gender infrastructures are being undermined. The role of training can be highlighted in this process, whereby assumptions have been made that "this set of technical skills of gender analysis, planning, and programming can be transferred to 'everyone'" (Davids and Van Eerdewijk 2016: 87). As Prügl (2011: 83) argues, gender training has been employed to produce the right inclination among bureaucrats towards the governance of gender, by seeking to increase the technical and administrative skills of professionals so that they become better programme administrators. Consequently, gender mainstreaming—and, more specifically, gender training—has tended to focus on an individualistic notion of change, overemphasising the capacity for individual change and denying the powerful forces at work which resist gender equality at the institutional level.

However, it is important to understand institutional resistance in order to clarify the blockages to gender training's potential to contribute to transformative change. As argued by Lut Mergaert in a 2015 UN Women Training Centre Virtual Dialogue on Resistances, three key indicators of institutional resistance can be identified:

1. The context of the training, e.g. if training is not part of a wider gender mainstreaming strategy, it may serve as an alibi for the organisation and indicate institutional resistance.
2. The immobility or unwillingness of an organisation to change, e.g. when those at the top want to maintain the status quo and do not allocate necessary resources to training.
3. The conditions and modalities of the training, e.g. if it is too short, lacks resources, or there is no space for negotiation to optimise training. Participant complaints of a lack of time, resources, and support can also denote institutional resistance (Mergaert, quoted in UN Women Training Centre 2015b).

This practical understanding is useful for conceptualising gender training processes within broader resistances to change. A further aspect to identify is the 'externalisation' of gendered change—that is, gender equality as a problem 'out there' and not 'in here', as discussed in more detail in Chapter 5. Davids and Van Eerdewijk (2016: 85) observe that, in the context of gender expertise in international development, the dialogue between partner and donor organisations "does not extend to debating donor's policymaking and priorities themselves." As Ferguson (2015: 387) argues:

> Gender becomes something that is only relevant in an organization's external activities, policies and programs. So, for example, while an institution might support a gender mainstreaming policy for a relevant sector or area of intervention, there may, at the same time, be high levels of resistance to any form of change in the operations and procedures of the institution itself.

This has substantive implications for gender training scenarios, as the majority of institutions do not prioritise gender mainstreaming and gender equality in their internal procedures and policies. A useful example to illustrate this point is the UN System Wide Action Plan on Gender Equality and the Empowerment of Women (UN-SWAP), as set out in Box 3.1.

Box 3.1 UN System Wide Action Plan on Gender Equality and the Empowerment of Women (UN-SWAP)

The UN-SWAP was endorsed by the United Nations Chief Executives Board for Coordination (CEB) in April 2012 and set 2017 as the target for the UN system to meet all its Performance Indicators. With its 15 commonly agreed-upon Performance Indicators (PIs), the UN-SWAP constitutes the first unified framework to systematically revitalise, capture, monitor and measure performance and accountability for the work of the UN system on gender equality and women's empowerment. All UN entities were expected to meet compliance on all 15 Performance Indicators by the end of 2017. However, as indicated by UN Women, this target is unlikely to be met, and the UN-SWAP reporting is expected to continue for the foreseeable future (UN Women 2013). Since its inception in 2012, progress has been made across most entities and Performance Indicators. For example, for the overall United Nations system, the proportion of ratings 'meeting' and 'exceeding' requirements increased from 31 to 64% between the first year of reporting, 2012 and 2016. However, while the proportion of reporting entities has increased by 18% since 2012, nearly 10% of entities still do not report on gender mainstreaming. It is interesting to note which Performance Indicators have seen the most progress. The top three indicators—Gender Responsive Auditing, Coherence and Knowledge Generation and Communication—are met by 90%, 88% and 86% of reporting entities, respectively. In contrast, the three worst performing indicators—Capacity Assessment, Gender Architecture and Resource Allocation—have registered little progress, and requirements are met by only 49%, 25% and 22% of entities in these areas, respectively (ibid.).

This example demonstrates that institutional resistance is often stronger in the areas of internal gender issues, and that this is consistent across the UN system Programmes and Funds and Specialized Agencies. In the context of gender training more specifically, resistance to discussing and addressing internal issues—as opposed to external or programme-focused aspects of gender equality—often arises at all stages of the training cycle. At the **Analysis and Planning** stage, initial discussions with those commissioning the training are key conditioning factors for the subsequent change process. As Lombardo and Mergaert (2016: 54) find, "many gender trainers consider support from the top levels in an organization as a condition for success in dealing with resistances when implementing gender mainstreaming and during gender training processes." Those who are directly involved in conditioning the training may have limited capacity to promote gender equality, depending on their position within institutional hierarchies and the overall institutional commitment to transformative gendered change. Implicit forms of institutional resistance to gender equality at this stage include "dedicating insufficient funds, time, and personnel to gender mainstreaming and training, to the exclusion of non-hegemonic voices, or the refusal to make certain pieces of information public. These may pose different constraints for gender trainers, including when negotiating the training activities with commissioners, for example, when agreeing on modalities such as the length of the training" (ibid.: 54). Such resistances at the commissioning/analysis and planning stage have a knock-on effect for the rest of the training cycle. For example, as found throughout the literature, training participants are more likely to be resistant during the training scenario when they are aware that support for gender equality and gender change are merely rhetorical, and that their institution does not have a substantive commitment to such change (Hansen-Pauly et al. 2009: 24; Mergaert and Demuynck 2011). This may take the form, for example, of the marginalisation of gender issues and activities. If gender is compartmentalised into one department or team, there is little incentive for staff across the organisation to take the issue seriously. For example, when training staff at the Association for Rural Advancement in South Africa, Bydawell (2010: 46) found that "some staff felt that the gender specialist was now 'doing gender' and this meant that they did not need to get involved with the issue themselves."

During the **Design and Development** stage, institutional resistances may be manifested when identifying the content and approach of the training, as discussed in more detail in Chapter 4. For the purposes of this chapter, certain challenges can be highlighted. For example, following the discussion of the *externalisation* of gender in/equality above, it may be difficult to include issues such as challenging male privilege in management structures; gender imbalance at different staffing levels of the organisation and internal policies and procedures. As highlighted in Chapter 2 and discussed in more detail in Chapter 4, requests for "technocratic fixes to the gender problem" are prevalent at this stage of the training cycle. As Ferguson (2015) notes:

> As often found in many different aspects of feminist practice, it is "okay" to talk about gender as long as nobody has to give anything up or be profoundly challenged about their assumptions, beliefs and behaviors. This can be said to function on an institutional, as well as a personal, level. It leads to gender being a "component" of policy and activities, but not an ongoing structural consideration in terms of the procedures and approaches of an institution – an integrationist rather than transformative approach. When gender can only be discussed as being external to an institution, it seems that gender expertise comes up against a wall. If we are unable to attack privilege and power, then how far can we get with increasing gender equality? Or, put more bluntly, if we cannot get the men at the top to accept a gender analysis and approach, then what is the point?

Leading on from the design and development phase, institutional resistances are also prevalent during the **Implementation** of training. Building on the individual resistances tackled in Chapter 2, such resistance is often triggered by feelings of incapacity by participants due to the specific constraints of their institutional context, rather than necessarily to the goal of gender equality. As identified by Lombardo and Mergaert (2016: 56):

> It might be difficult for a trainer to empirically distinguish this kind of incapacity from 'genuine' resistance to gender equality during a training session. Nonetheless, it is possible when considering the elements included at the planning stage of a specific gender mainstreaming initiative. If the resources (funding, personnel, time) or skills (training, expert consulting) needed to implement gender mainstreaming have not been foreseen in the planning of the action, actors are likely to feel ill equipped to fulfil their tasks, and thus are likely to prove resistant to gender change.

Institutional resistances and limitations have a strong impact on the potential for gender-transformative **Evaluation**, as discussed in more detail below. If internal issues and power dynamics are not key aspects of the design and development of the training, it will not be possible to evaluate the extent to which the training has contributed to broader processes of transformative change across an organisation. These challenges that may manifest themselves at different stages in the training cycle are mapped in Fig. 3.1.

A key question for transformative gender training is how to best approach and engage with institutional resistances? As argued in

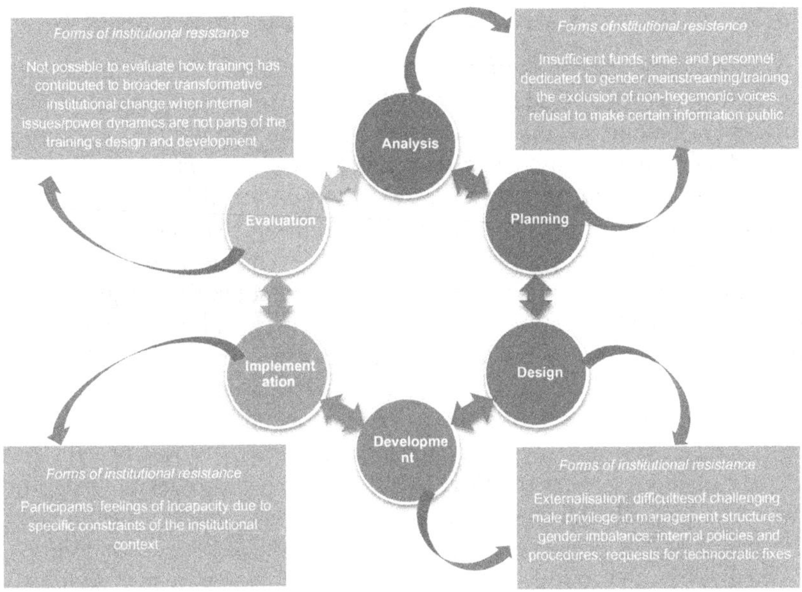

Fig. 3.1 Diagram of training cycle and institutional resistances (*Source* Author's own design based on the UN Women Training Centre's Training Cycle)

Chapter 2, resistances are a key part of the contestation process, which is essential for gender training contributing to transformative change for gender equality. However, what strategies and tools can gender trainers employ for dealing with these institutional resistances at different stages in the training cycle? Maitrayee Mokhupadhyay, for example—during the UN Women Training Centre's Virtual Dialogue on Resistances (2015b)—proposed two key strategies for trainers: to focus on the core business of the institution commissioning the training and ensure that trainers are knowledgeable about the sector they are dealing with; and to assert autonomy in the face of interventionism by institutions. These questions are explored in more depth in Chapter 5, which discusses innovative techniques and 'ways of being' for moving gender training forward. I now go on to explore different ways in which feminist change can be understood in the context of gender training.

Feminist Theories of Transformative Change

Understanding the kinds of change which gender training can contribute helps to shape realistic objectives for the outcomes of gender training processes. Change at a number of levels can be highlighted here—from individual/behavioural change to societal change, as set out in Fig. 3.2. In terms of individual change, research from the field of behavioural studies is useful for gender training, highlighting that successful change must be guided through social interaction—"change is more sustainable when it is driven by conditions that invite people to engage in social learning" (Hord and Roussin 2013: 3). Thus, gender training can be understood as a site of 'social learning', in which trainers "facilitate the conversations that invite others to own the desired change" (ibid.). A number of different approaches can be used to understand what triggers individual behavioural change. However, for the purposes of exploring change through gender training, it is also important to acknowledge the ways in which an individual's knowledge, actions and view of the world are based on his or her experiences (Freire 1992). Freire, for example, highlights the dialectical nature of the relationship between *consciousness of* and *action upon* reality, both of which are required for the transforming act of *praxis* (Allsup 2003).

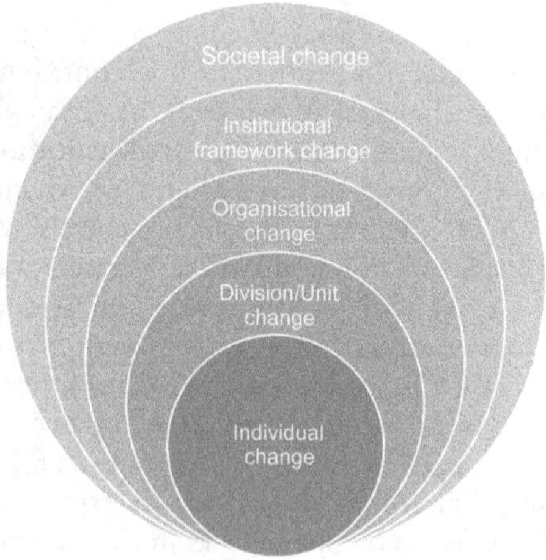

Fig. 3.2 Levels of change through gender training (*Source* UN Women Training Centre 2017b)

This relates to more social understandings of behavioural change, such as Bandura's 'Social Learning Theory'. In this approach, behaviour is understood to be learned through experience and observation. In turn, this leads to the behaviour of others being modelled and the consequence of those behaviours either reinforcing or deterring the future repetition of such behaviour. This is useful for gender training, as it suggests that certain attitudes and behaviours are not inevitable. Rather these are learned and, as such, can be 'un-learned' through training and education. Particularly helpful for understanding change in terms of gender training is Myra Marx Ferree's Knowledge, Desire, Ability (KDA) approach (UN Women Training Centre 2017b). She sets out three core elements of the discursive change on which gender training is focused, as set out in Fig. 3.3:

- Knowledge (K) on the desired change;
- Desire (D) or motivation (what is valued, feared, desired, etc.); and
- Abilities (A) (of articulation, reflection, communication) to make the change occur.

These core elements, sometimes dubbed being "ready, willing and able" to make a transition (Lesthaeghe and Vanderhoeft 2001), are central to strategic planning for change. In order to contribute to social change, gender training must go beyond a focus on merely one or two of these aspects and engage with all three—that is, it must "engage trainees in restructuring their existing KDA systems" (UN Women Training Centre 2017b). Box 3.2, demonstrates why a focus on all three KDA aspects is so essential for gender training.

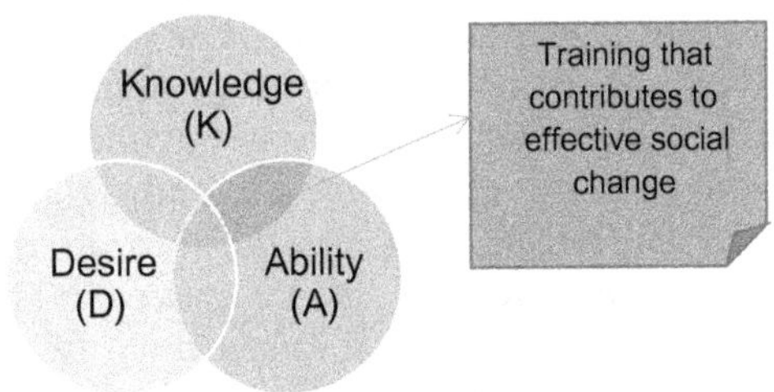

Fig. 3.3 KDA approach to change (*Source* UN Women Training Centre 2017b)

Box 3.2 Examples of why a KDA approach Is important for gender training

If gender training fosters knowledge (K) alone, it produces 'trained people' who are aware of facts related to gender equality, but are unlikely to have the desire (D) or ability (A) to transform their daily lives, work spaces or communities. If training equips trainees with knowledge (K) and abilities (A)—such as technical skills on gender—but does not support their desire (D) to engage in transformative change, it will not impact their commitment to transformation. If training endows participants with knowledge (K) and a desire (D) for gender change, but does not support their abilities (A) to engage in such change, it is likely to merely 'increase frustration'. Training that focuses on abilities/skills (A) and desire/commitment (D) but is not grounded in knowledge (K) deprives trainees of the facts and information they will need to put these skills and commitment into practice (UN Women Training Centre 2017b).

As such, it appears that gender training which leads to change addresses all three components of a KDA approach, that is, training which increases knowledge *and* a desire to learn, as well as offering the ability to challenge gender through skills or access to networks of knowers (UN Women Training Centre 2017b).

In terms of institutional change, the field of feminist institutionalism is useful for the theory and practice of gender training. Recent research in this area explores "how institutional change happens and how feminist strategies of claims making and inclusion can impact processes of institutional change" (Mackay and Waylen 2014: 490). Feminist institutionalism is concerned with *how* institutions can be changed and draws on "more dynamic conceptions of institutional change, emphasizing the subtle and often gradual ways in which institutions evolve over time as a result of both exogenous and endogenous factors" (Mackay et al. 2010: 577). For feminist institutionalism, individual and institutional changes are dialectic. Rather than being separate processes, they are closely interwoven, reinforcing and influencing one another (ibid.). By acknowledging that institutional power relations are deeply historical and constantly evolving, feminist institutional approaches explore how such processes are susceptible to agency, change and transformation (Kenny 2007). For the purposes of this book, my concern is specifically the role that gender training can play in such processes. Within this understanding, institutions can be seen as sites of ongoing political struggle, conflicts and coalitions, in which change occurs *in specific historical contexts marked by multiple shifting interests and alliances* (ibid.).

A number of further insights from the field of feminist institutionalism are useful for understanding the relationship between gender training and change (adapted from Kenny 2007; Mackay and Waylen 2014; Mackay et al. 2010; Mackay 2014). For example, the concept of 'gendered nested newness' helps to understand "which specific elements of a given institutional arrangement are (or are not) renegotiable, and why some aspects are more amenable to change than others" (Thelen 2004: 36; Mackay 2014) in gender training processes. In addition, it is important to pay attention to both *endogenous sources of institutional change and stasis*—including dynamics of institutional power relations, resistance and reproduction (Kenny 2011)—and *external change drivers*, in particular the impact of changes in the wider gender order within institutional environments (Waylen 2007). Further reflection would be useful here in terms of what this means for gender training and the extent to which such interventions can be understood as endogenous or external. This brief overview on the insights of social learning theory, a KDA approach and feminist institutionalism maps onto the discussion of resistances, above and in Chapter 2, in which both individual and institutional aspects of resistances are taken into account. The chapter now turns to Theory of Change approaches, which represent a pragmatic, yet still political, tool for maximising gender training's potential to contribute to transformative change.

Theory of Change and Evaluation

Theory of Change approaches are a pragmatic yet political tool for maximising the potential of gender training to contribute to transformative change, and can help to operationalise some of the theoretical discussions outlined above. In particular, such an approach offers three concrete contributions to the field: clarifying assumptions and "identifying the intermediary steps" and "specific outputs that a programme or intervention can realistically anticipate" (Cohen et al. 2013); identifying "entry points, risks and opportunities" specific to the institutional context and "proposing an explicit Theory of Change that explains how gender training interventions could contribute to the organisational goals" (ibid.: 30); and developing "hypotheses and consensus on how gender training is supposed to work in a specific programme or intervention; how stakeholders view the need for change; and how they perceive the actual changes" (ibid.: 32). Theory of Change approaches have been prevalent in the field of gender equality in recent years, but to date there is little work specifically from the field of gender training, with two key exceptions. First, NGO Promundo has developed a Theory of Change that applies to their training programmes. Key insights from their work include that a Theory of Change for gender training should be built upon considerations of structures and power relations in society; it should incorporate a theory of group learning in order to contribute to transformative and sustainable change; and that theories of learning are particularly important when the learning objectives of the training include critical reflection and attitude change (Promundo et al. 2013). Second, the UN Women Training Centre (2017b) proposes a model for Theory of Change in gender training, which incorporates:

> An exploration of institutional history and power relations, as well as and explicit analysis of power relations and resistances. This allows for training initiatives to be located within a wider analysis of how change comes about, while acknowledging the wider systems and actors that influence change. (ibid.: 21)

While the UN Women Training Centre's Theory of Change approach is a useful contribution, three issues can be highlighted at this stage in terms of its practical application to the contemporary theory and practice of gender training. First, as set out in Chapter 1, there are currently no agreed quality standards or guidelines for the field. This means that a Theory of Change approach is not widely adopted or considered in most current gender training processes. Second, as Theory of Change approaches are relatively new to gender training, there is limited experience of how to put these into practice and integrate them more substantively into the Training Cycle and overall training process. As such, how can gender trainers work to develop a more substantive and explicit approach to Theory of Change and begin to apply this more systematically across the field?

A final concern with the use of Theory of Change approaches is the under-development of evaluation in the field of gender training, especially compared with the broader field of gender-sensitive or gender-transformative evaluation. This is a problem, as there is currently little understanding or evidence of the specific contributions that gender training makes to transformative change more broadly. To date, approaches to the evaluation of gender training have tended to focus more on the evaluation of *the training itself*, rather than the *impact* of the training. In large part, this is due to the difficulty of discerning the specific impact or long-term results of training, since change is not generated by training in isolation. However, as argued in the recent UN Women Training Centre (2018) paper on evaluation:

> If evaluations are to contribute to training's transformative potential, they must adhere to a methodological approach based on feminist and participatory values and the deconstruction of power relations.

In response, the paper argues for a *gender-transformative approach* to evaluation, with a focus on how gender and power relationships change as a result of the training. Such an approach also supports training participants and other stakeholders to be empowered by the evaluation process itself (ibid.). Following the overarching argument of this book, I argue that a *feminist evaluation* approach is required for *feminist gender training*. This draws on the work of Podems and Negroustoueva (2016) who highlight the reflective nature of feminist evaluation. As Hay (2012) argues, feminist evaluation is "a way of understanding how gender and other intersecting social cleavages (such as race, class, sexuality, caste and religion) define and shape the experience and exercise of power in different contexts." At its core, feminist evaluation involves a recognition of the political nature of evaluation and acknowledges different ways of knowing. Feminist evaluators are also cautious about the limits to a Monitoring and Evaluation approach, which posits that "everything should be measured, can be measured, that measurement will enhance our ability to improve, change, replicate, and that change is predictable—we will know what it is like, where it will occur, when and how to assess it." As such, uncertainty and reflexivity are key to the practice of feminist evaluation.

Box 3.3: Challenges for evaluation in gender training
A recent Virtual Dialogue conducted by the UN Women Community of Practice in Training for Gender Equality (2017a) explored some of the key challenges for evaluation in this field:

- Processes of training and capacity development 'are not linear but involve an often messy and incremental, step by step, sometimes going backwards, change' (Walters 2007).
- Training can only contribute to change if both internal and external organisational aspects are taken into consideration.
- Institutional change through training requires the creation of a whole 'gender system' by which gender awareness and transformative change become ingrained in the organisation's 'DNA'.
- There is a relationship between individual and institutional changes. For instance, when gender training targets staff members in an organisation, it targets people as individuals but also starts a collective dynamic that can influence people's private lives, workplaces and communities.
- While individual change can influence institutional change, and vice versa, this relationship is not automatic. Translating individual change into institutional change, for example, requires an organisation to be supportive of gender training and to enable staff to apply their new knowledge across the organisation's external *and* internal dimensions. This could entail encouraging staff to discuss and seek to transform the organisation's internal gender culture, while applying their new skills to external projects (UN Women Training Centre 2013).

Following this discussion, how can feminist evaluation principles be applied to gender training scenarios, particularly given the multiple constraints and contradictions highlighted throughout the book? While feminist approaches to evaluation have been developed in other fields, to date there has been little substantive work in terms of gender training. A recent paper by UN Women Training aims to provide a conceptual and methodological framework for 'gender-transformative' evaluation of gender training. A number of key arguments from the paper can be highlighted here. The first is that evaluation needs to be integrated into all stages of the training cycle, and not left for the 'final' stage. According to UN Women Training Centre, this requires:

> A new way of thinking about evaluating training that engages more explicitly with power dynamics and institutional change/resistance/inertia. This means that the evaluation of training for gender equality will only be gender-transformative if such an approach guides all stages of the training cycle.

Second, the paper argues that evaluation of gender training needs to move beyond the first three levels of the Kirkpatrick model—Reaction, Learning and Behaviour—and focus more explicitly on the final level, Results. This involves exploring how the training interacts with and contributes to broader change processes in gender equality within the organisation and analysing the key power dynamics at play in facilitating or impeding the impact of the training on transformative change for gender equality. In practice, this means that the most basic evaluation tools—such as questionnaires—can be developed along gender-transformative lines:

> Such tools can then be used to more effectively assess the impact of the training on participants, as well as to situate the training much more specifically within broader institutional change processes. This means the power dynamics of both the training process and other processes of individual and institutional change are highlighted and engaged with from the outset.

Next, the paper argues that participatory evaluation needs to be built into the training process, "developing a co-creation process which facilitates participation and critical reflection on existing power dynamics and the possibilities of change." That is, evaluation should be conducted by engaging the feminist pedagogical principles outlined in Chapter 4 of this book. Finally, it highlights the importance of a follow-up stage to the evaluation and the need to involve a wide range of stakeholders in this. In practical terms, this involves analysing multiple levels of change, identifying indicators of sustainability and following up by supporting participants to implement expected changes and by documenting their experiences. In addition to these key arguments, the paper offers a range of tools and methods for evaluating the different levels.

The inclusion of concrete, practical guidelines thus makes this paper an important contribution to the debate on evaluating gender training. However, I would argue that we are in a very early stage of applying feminist evaluation principles and practice to gender training. To date, evaluation has not been a priority issue for the field, and as such there has been very little reflection or documentation of evaluation theory and practice. While those interested in feminist gender training are naturally concerned with understanding the impact of training on broader change processes, the role of evaluation in this is currently under-theorised. Moreover, real challenges exist in implementing feminist evaluation principles in gender training scenarios. As highlighted throughout the book, gender training processes tend to be time bound and budget bound, requiring a creative approach to maximising the impact of such scenarios. What more work needs to be done in order to cultivate and systematically integrate feminist evaluation principles into the practice of gender training?

Conclusions

As this chapter has argued, the relationship between gender training and transformative change is not clearly articulated at present. A number of different ways of improving our understanding of such a relationship are outlined above. The concept of *institutional resistances* is a useful addition to the *individual resistances*, discussed in Chapter 2. By exploring the specific context of institutional power dynamics and other change processes, we can have a better understanding of the ways in which gender training is located. Moreover, an analysis of persistent and enduring resistances to gender equality helps to contextualise the challenges of gender training processes and scenarios, and to be more clear about the kinds of change to which these can contribute. This chapter's review of the literature on change—exploring both individual and institutional changes—particularly highlights feminist institutionalism as an area that can be developed further from the perspective of gender training, to understand the ways in which training processes interact with dynamics and levels of gendered change within institutions. The exploration of a Theory of Change approach for gender training outlines the work done to date, especially by the UN Women Training Centre. Nevertheless, it notes that this methodology is currently under-explored and under-utilised, and could be integrated more systematically into gender training processes in order to articulate more clearly the specific ways in which gender training is hoped, or expected, to contribute to transformative change processes. In addition, the lack of a substantive approach to gender-transformative evaluation for gender training limits our understanding of the impact of such processes in the short, medium and long term.

It is important to continue to delineate and acknowledge the limitations of gender training in order not to overstate its role and contribution. For example, the notion of 'bounded change within an existing system', elaborated upon by Mackay (2014), is helpful for understanding change through gender training, as it helps to set realistic and manageable targets and indicators for change. The purpose of this book is to highlight the ways in which the potential of gender training as a transformative tool can be maximised. Even without perfect conditions, gender trainers can work to maximise the spaces for feminist change within the existing constraints and conditions. For example, this involves viewing gender training as a site for challenging institutional resistance and/or inertia. In this reading, gender training can be seen as a 'moment' of rupture or disturbance in institutional change processes. As argued in the following chapter, feminist pedagogical principles and practices offer the strongest possibilities for gender training to convert these 'moments' into opportunities for contributing to transformative change.

References

Allsup, R. E. (2003). Praxis and the Possible: Thoughts on the Writings of Maxine Greene and Paulo Freire. *Philosophy of Music Education Review, 11*(2), 157–169.

Batliwala, S. (2012). *Changing Their World: Concepts and Practices of Women's Movements* (2nd ed.). Toronto: Association for Women's Rights in Development (AWID). Available at http://www.awid.org/sites/default/files/atoms/files/changing_their_world_2ed_full_eng.pdf.

Bustelo, M., Ferguson, L., & Forest, M. (2016). Introduction. In M. Bustelo, L. Ferguson, & M. Forest (Eds.), *The Politics of Feminist Knowledge Transfer: Gender Training and Gender Expertise* (pp. 1–24). London: Palgrave Macmillan.

Bydawell, M. (2010). AFRA Confronts Gender Issues: The Process of Creating a Gender Strategy. *Gender & Development, 5*(1), 43–48. https://doi.org/10.1080/741922299.

Cohen, S. I., Sachdeva, N., Taylor, S. J., & Cortes, P. (2013, April 30–May 3). *Expert Group Meeting: Gender Mainstreaming Approaches in Development Programming: Being Strategic and Achieving Results in an Evolving Development*

Context, Santo Domingo, Dominican Republic. Santo Domingo: UN Women. Available at http://www.unwomen.org/~/media/Headquarters/Attachments/Sections/How%20We%20Work/UNSystemCoordination/FINAL%20EGM%20REPORT%201%20NOV%20version%20pdf.pdf.

Daly, M. (2005). Gender Mainstreaming in Theory and Practice. *Social Politics: International Studies in Gender, State and Society, 12*(2), 433–450.

Davids, T., & Van Eerdewijk, A. (2016). The Smothering of Feminist Knowledge: Gender Mainstreaming Articulated Through Neoliberal Governmentalities. In M. Bustelo, L. Ferguson, & M. Forest (Eds.), *The Politics of Feminist Knowledge Transfer* (pp. 80–98). Abingdon and New York: Palgrave Macmillan.

Eyben, R., Kidder, T., Rowlands, J., & Bronstein, A. (2008). Thinking About Change for Development Practice: A Case Study from Oxfam UK. *Development in Practice, 18*(2), 201–212.

Ferguson, L. (2015). 'This Is Our Gender Person': The Messy Business of Working as a Gender Expert in International Development. *International Feminist Journal of Politics, 17*(3), 380–397.

Freire, P. (1992). *Pedagogy of Hope: Reliving Pedagogy of the Oppressed.* New York: Continuum.

Hansen-Pauly, M. A., Bentner, G., Jovanovic, V., & Zerbato, D. (2009). *CLIL Across Contexts: A Scaffolding Framework for CLIL Teacher Education.* Luxembourg: University of Luxembourg.

Hay, K. (2012). Engendering Policies and Programs Through Feminist Evaluation: Opportunities and Insights. *Indian Journal of Gender Studies, 19*(2), 321–340.

Hord, S. M., & Roussin, J. L. (2013). Introduction. In S. M. Hord & J. L. Roussin (Eds.), *Implementing Change Through Learning: Concerns-Based Concepts, Tools, and Strategies for Guiding Change* (1st ed., pp. 1–7). Corwin: Thousand Oaks.

Kenny, M. (2007). Gender, Institutions and Power A Critical Review. *Politics, 27*(2), 91–100.

Kenny, M. (2011). Gender and Institutions of Political Recruitment: Candidate Selection in Post-devolution Scotland. In M. L. Krook & F. Mackay (Eds.), *Gender, Politics and Institutions* (pp. 21–41). Basingstoke: Palgrave Macmillan.

Lesthaeghe, R., & Vanderhoeft, C. (2001). Ready, Willing and Able—A Conceptualization of Transitions to New Behavioral Forms. In J. B. Casterline (Ed.), *US National Research Council: Diffusion Processes and Fertility Transition* (pp. 240–264). Washington, DC: National Academies Press.

Lombardo, E., & Mergaert, L. (2016). Resistance in Gender Training and Mainstreaming Processes. In M. Bustelo, L. Ferguson, & M. Forest (Eds.), *The Politics of Feminist Knowledge Transfer: Gender Training and Gender Expertise* (pp. 43–61). Abingdon and New York: Palgrave Macmillan.

Mackay, F. (2014). Nested Newness, Institutional Innovation, and the Gendered Limits of Change. *Politics & Gender, 10*(4), 549–571.

Mackay, F., & Waylen, G. (2014). Introduction: Gendering 'New' Institutions. *Politics & Gender, 10*(4), 489–494.

Mackay, F., Kenny, M., & Chappell, L. (2010). New Institutionalism Through a Gender Lens: Towards a Feminist Institutionalism? *International Political Science Review, 31*(5), 573–588.

Mergaert, L., & Demuynck, K. (2011). *The Ups and Downs of Gender Mainstreaming in the EU Research Policy—The Gender Toolkit and Training Activities in FP7.* Antwerp: Policy Research Centre on Equal Opportunities.

Mukhopadhyay, M., & Wong, F. (2007). Introduction: Revisiting Gender Training. The Making and Remaking of Gender Knowledge. In Franz Wong & Maitrayee Mukhopadhyay (Eds.), *Revisiting Gender Training: The Making and Remaking of Gender Knowledge—A Global Sourcebook.* Amsterdam, The Netherlands: KIT Royal Tropical Institute. Available at http://213ou636sh0ptphd141fqei1.wpengine.netdna-cdn.com/gender/wp-content/uploads/publications/1031_Gender-revisiting-web2.pdf.

Podems, D., & Negroustoueva, S. (2016). *Feminist Evaluation. Better Evaluation.* Available at http://www.betterevaluation.org/approaches/feminist_evaluation.

Promundo, Instituto PAPAI, Salud y Género and ECOS. (2013). *Program H|M|D: A Toolkit for Action/Engaging Youth to Achieve Gender Equity.* Rio de Janeiro and Washington, DC: Promundo. Available at http://promundoglobal.org/wp-content/uploads/2015/01/Program-HMD-Toolkit-for-Action.pdf.

Prügl, E. (2011). Diversity Management and Gender Mainstreaming as Technologies of Government. *Politics and Gender, 7*, 71–89.

Thelen, K. (2004). *How Institutions Evolve: The Political Economy of Skills in Germany, Britain, the United States and Japan.* Cambridge and New York: Cambridge University Press.

UN Women. (2013). *UN-SWAP: A Plan to Improve Gender Equality and the Empowerment of Women Across the UN System.* New York: UN Women. Available at http://www.unwomen.org/en/how-we-work/un-system-coordination/promoting-un-accountability.

UN Women Training Centre. (2013, July 1–19). *Virtual Dialogue Report: Evaluation of Training for Gender Equality.* Santo Domingo: UN Women Training Centre. Available at https://trainingcentre.unwomen.org/mod/page/view.php?id=2145.

UN Women Training Centre. (2015a). Training For Gender Equality: Twenty Years On. *Santo Domingo*, p. 41. Available at https://trainingcentre.unwomen.org/pluginfile.php/72/mod_data/content/18873/Paper_TrainingForGenderEquality%2B20-B%20(8).pdf.

UN Women Training Centre. (2015b, May 6–13). *Virtual Dialogue on Resistances in Training for Gender Equality*. Available at https://trainingcentre.unwomen.org/mod/page/view.php?id=2119.

UN Women Training Centre. (2016). *Compendium of Good Practices in Training for Gender Equality*. Santo Domingo: UN Women Training Centre. Available at https://trainingcentre.unwomen.org/pluginfile.php/72/mod_data/content/26773/COMPENDIO_ONU-M-WEB.pdf.

UN Women Training Centre. (2017a, April 24–May 19). *Final Report: Virtual Dialogue on Understanding Change Through Training for Gender Equality*. Santo Domingo: UN Women Training Centre.

UN Women Training Centre. (2017b). *Working Paper Series: A Theory of Change for Training for Gender Equality*. Prepared by Dr. Lucy Ferguson. Santo Domingo: UN Women Training Centre. Available at https://trainingcentre.unwomen.org/pluginfile.php/72/mod_data/content/40218/01%20Theory%20of%20Change.pdf.

UN Women Training Centre. (2018). *Gender-Transformative Evaluation of Training for Gender Equality*. Santo Domingo: UN Women Training Centre.

Walters, H. (2007). *Capacity Development, Institutional Change and Theory of Change: What Do We Mean and Where Are the Linkages*, p. 11. Available at http://portals.wi.wur.nl/files/docs/successfailuredevelopment/Walters_CapacityDevelopmentConceptPaperFIN.pdf.

Waylen, G. (2007). *Engendering Transitions*. Oxford: Oxford University Press.

CHAPTER 4

Gender Training and Feminist Pedagogies

Abstract An important aspect of maximising the transformative potential of gender training is the application of feminist pedagogical principles throughout all aspects of the training process. This is explored in detail in this chapter, which discusses not just feminist pedagogical principles, but also what makes a *feminist gender trainer*. This chapter also highlights a range of unresolved and unfinished issues within the field of gender training, especially when it comes to implementing feminist pedagogical principles—in particular the tensions between technocratic demands and feminist politics and practice. It is argued that feminist gender training requires individual, collective and institutional 'transformative courage' in the face of such challenges.

Keywords Critical pedagogies · Reflexivity · Feminist gender trainers
Methodologies

So far, this book has been concerned with key critiques of gender training; challenges in gender training and exploring the possibilities for gender training to contribute to change. In this chapter, I explore the ways in which feminist pedagogical principles and practices can work to overcome some of these challenges and maximise the contribution of gender training to transformative change for gender equality. Gender training has its roots in feminist pedagogies from adult education, which draw from three key strands. First, critical pedagogies developed

L. Ferguson, *Gender Training*, Gender and Politics,
https://doi.org/10.1007/978-3-319-91827-3_4

by Paulo Freire and others, adhering to the view that: "Besides being an act of knowing, education is also a political act. That is why no pedagogy is neutral" (Freire and Shore 1987: 13). As argued throughout this book, if training is to address hierarchies and privilege, then it must also be considered a 'political act'. Second, aspects of feminist pedagogies originate from the exercises of experience sharing in women's community groups during the women's liberation movement, which can be related to 'awareness raising and consciousness building' (UN Women Training Centre 2016b: 24) activities in gender training (Haraway 1991). Third—and perhaps most importantly—feminist pedagogies have been developed in relation to the teaching of women's and gender studies in university environments, to ensure that feminist theories and practices inform such teaching. While there are some key differences between gender training and feminist adult education, a number of similarities and overlaps between the two fields can be identified, such as drawing on feminist movements and understandings of learning, activism and transformative change; being guided by feminist pedagogical principles; and having the potential to take place over long-term periods and build strong rapport among learners, facilitators and groups of learners (UN Women Training Centre 2017c).

Building on these foundations, a number of core aspects of feminist pedagogies for gender training can be identified. The UN Women Training Centre (2017a) outlines four key principles specifically for gender training: participatory learning; the validation of personal experience; the encouragement of social justice, activism and accountability; and the development of critical thinking and open-mindedness. The objective of this chapter is to develop the work already done in this area, specifically by drawing on practice in order to illuminate some of the intricate challenges and possibilities of gender training scenarios. The first section outlines the four feminist pedagogical principles proposed by UN Women Training Centre in more detail, reflecting on the challenges of applying these in practice and highlighting specific challenges for training. Next, the chapter proposes a range of tools and techniques for addressing these challenges. Following this, it explores what specific qualities and skills might be required for the making of *feminist gender* trainers. This recalls the discussions of professionalisation and quality in Chapter 1, which are further elaborated in Chapter 5. In the conclusions, I discuss the remaining unresolved issues and tensions highlighted in the chapter.

Reflecting on the Application of Feminist Pedagogical Principles

As argued by UN Women Training Centre (2017a), feminist pedagogical principles are "underpinned by a commitment to a feminist critique (which challenges the basis of all knowledge and ways of knowing) and a feminist project (which aims to transform oppressive and interlocking power relations in pursuit of a world characterized by increased social justice)" (Manicom 1992: 366–367). As such, feminist pedagogies view learning "through the lens of oppression and attempts to look at racial, sexual, and social diversity and inequality" (Rajani 2015: 8). They are driven by the "need to understand how patriarchal ideology has truncated and distorted our knowledge and experiences of ourselves and the world" (Martel and Peterat 1998: 82). They aim to "liberate the student from the traditional patriarchal traps of the classroom" (Janus n.d.: 1). Here, I explore how each key principle of feminist pedagogies can be applied to the practice of gender training and the specific dilemmas and tensions that training processes may generate, and propose ways of overcoming some of these challenges.

First, feminist learning processes are *participatory* and involve the feminist pedagogue 'decentring' authority and remaining a learner in the classroom (Stanley-Spaeth 2000). Participatory learning takes place in the 'feminist classroom'—a particular kind of feminist learning space which is "collaborative, experiential, egalitarian, interactive, empowering, relational and affective," with the aim of supporting students to become sympathetic to the concerns of critical feminist pedagogy (Gajjala et al. 2010: 415). In addition, feminist pedagogies call for sensitivity to gender, race, class, sexuality, disability, multiculturalism, postcolonial criticism and globalisation (Wicker et al. 2005). Here it is useful to recall hooks' concept of a 'democratic classroom' (hooks 1994), one which "challenges the fundamental assumptions of hierarchical education, where everyone's presence is affirmed and valued" and in which teachers must "move attention away from … [their] own voice and towards that of … [their] students" (Penn 1997). Palmer's (1993) notion of 'hospitality' is also useful here. He suggests that "a learning space needs to be hospitable not to make learning painless but to make the painful things possible, things without which no learning can occur — things like exposing ignorance, testing tentative hypotheses, challenging false or partial information and mutual criticism of thought." Moreover, as

Jackson argues, in the hospitable classroom "students are actively invited in rather than just neutrally tolerated, and challenges to the coherence of particular identities are advanced gently, respectfully, and in a spirit of mutual humility" (Jackson 2016).

A number of issues can be highlighted in terms of implementing participatory learning in gender training. For example, to what extent can gender training scenarios be called 'feminist classrooms'? What are the challenges involved in constructing online 'feminist classrooms' (as discussed below). What needs to done in gender training to create learning environments that are "collaborative, experiential, egalitarian, interactive, empowering, relational and affective?" (Gajjala et al. 2010). One key aspect of this is for trainers to work as 'feminist pedagogues', working at all times in a dual role as facilitator and learner. To what extent is this kind of role compatible with the specific contexts of training scenarios? In which kinds of scenarios might this be more challenging? It is also important to acknowledge the power dynamics of training scenarios, in which hierarchies may not be as straightforward as in a teacher–student situation. In some cases, it may be the trainer who is perceived to be at a power disadvantage vis-à-vis the training participants, due to intersecting power dynamics such as gender, class, age, nationality, race/ethnicity and nationality. Flood (2011: 150), for example, explores how:

> men's presence as students in feminist classrooms poses challenges to traditional constructions of feminist pedagogy and can generate patriarchal forms of relating and resistance. Yet, their involvement can prompt their personal and intellectual transformation, without significantly compromising similar transformations among female students.

How can awareness of the sometimes complex and contradictory nature of these dynamics be built into the gender training process? How can ideas around 'pedagogy for the privileged' or 'education for the privileged'—developed in the fields of critical masculinity studies and whiteness studies—be incorporated into designing gender training in these kinds of contexts?

The *validation of personal experience* is an essential component of feminist gender training. This means encouraging participants to share from their own personal and professional knowledge, in order to link personal experience with institutional structures of subordination and to understand personal experience as political, historical and socially constructed

(Gajjala et al. 2010). The validation of personal experience raises some specific challenges for gender training. For example, in many gender training scenarios, participants' 'personal experience' can come into tension with feminist ideas. For example, Lombardo and Mergaert highlight challenges such as the 'myth of equality' (Lombardo and Mergaert 2016). That is, if participants *perceive* that gender equality is not a problem for their organisation—or themselves as individuals—then it is difficult for gender trainers to challenge these perceptions. As such, trainers need to be skilled and develop strategies to "manage the proliferation of experience-based knowledge claims and avoid the anti-democratic tendency to see experiential claims to know (especially to know about oppression) as sacrosanct" (Sanchez-Casal and MacDonald 2002). This requires a dual process of respecting personal knowledge while finding tools to challenge the basis of such knowledge claims, and how these may come into tension with the experiences of other participants with different identities and positionalities. These concerns may be of particular relevance when training the powerful, particularly if participants are highly resistant to ideas about gender equality. Lombardo and Mergaert (2016) show how training participants may often demonstrate a "resistance to learn something from a feminist." This can put trainers in a difficult position, as their audience will "often be ill-disposed to any message simply because of their role as gender trainers" (ibid.: 67–68). Intersectionality is a key concept here for engaging the different experiences of participants through exploring their positionality in the multiple hierarchies of gender, class, ethnicity, age, nationality, etc., as discussed in Chapters 2 and 5. The dynamics of the learning environment are also important here. Which participants are able to speak out and which are not? Which aspects of experience are voiced and validated, and which are marginalised?

Feminist pedagogies are grounded in the *encouragement of social justice, activism and accountability*, rooted in feminist consciousness-raising groups of the 1960s and 1970s (Hoffman and Stake 2001). In terms of gender training, this means translating feminist principles into the transformation of institutions. bell hooks' concept of 'engaged pedagogy', for instance, emphasises well-being which "involves a knowledge of oneself and an accountability for one's actions" (Berila 2016). Learning processes guided by feminist pedagogical principles must hold learners, facilitators and institutions accountable for their attitudes, behaviours and practices/actions. However, as discussed in Chapter 2, one of the key challenges of contemporary gender training is resisting the technocratic pull, and grounding practice in a feminist politics of transformation. As such, what happens when these two aspects come into tension? For example, how can training participants be encouraged and supported to acknowledge accountability and take responsibility for gender equality in their institutions? How can gender training scenarios best be designed and implemented in order to negotiate individual and institutional resistances to change, when participants do not consider that gender equality to be relevant or important to their overall role? How can bell hooks' call for the feminist classroom as "a place where there is a sense of struggle" be applied to gender training, especially in an increasingly technocratic context?

Finally, feminist pedagogies involve the *development of critical thinking and open-mindedness.* As Kelly (2015) argues, "teachers and trainers commit to guiding learners to become independent thinkers who can use 'gender' as a critical lens to examine power, social constructions of expertise and what constitutes 'knowledge'." In order to be able to explore the 'personal experience' discussed above, learners must be able to compare and evaluate evidence from diverse standpoints and experiences, and to be open to changing one's own perspective and opinions in light of these comparisons. Critical thinking, therefore, is "both dialogical and dialectical, and requires tolerance for ambiguity and difference as learners engage with diverse others" (ibid.). As Miller (2005: 36) suggests, feminist pedagogies "introduce into the classroom a plethora of possibilities that resist easy answers and disallow the maintenance of homogenous neatness." However, as the discussion above and Chapter 2 suggest, what happens when the goals of critical thinking and open-mindedness meet technocratic and bureaucratic cultures and institutions? For instance, a recent KIT paper points out that gender training often:

> implies packaging gender in ways that do not offend participants, which contributes to a sanitizing of what is essentially a political subject. This binary – between theoretical knowledge and practical knowledge – is a false dichotomy particularly from a feminist context and the notion of praxis: the iterative knowledge development process resulting from the interaction of theory and practice. Theory is developed from practice and subsequently used to further develop theory. In other words, theory and practice are not binary opposites but constitutive of feminist knowledge production. (Wong et al. 2016: 10)

In these scenarios, what can be done to maximise the space for critical thinking, even when the focus of the training may be predominantly technical, or focussed on specific results or outcomes? How can we cultivate 'tolerance for ambiguity' (Kelly 2015: 13) and resist 'homogenous neatness'? (Miller 2005: 36).

Feminist Pedagogies in Online Training

Having set out the general challenges that arise in applying feminist pedagogical principles to gender training, I now go on to explore in detail the implications of these tensions in online training settings. As online—and mobile—learning in gender equality continues to grow, it is important to explore the specific challenges and opportunities of delivering such content in an online environment. A key example of the prevalence of online training is UN Women's *I Know Gender* course. This self-paced online course offers an introduction to key concepts, international framework and methods related to gender equality, with the aim of developing participants' awareness and understanding of gender equality and women's empowerment "as a first step towards behavioural change and the integration of a gender perspective into everyday work," particularly of UN staff (UN Women Training Centre n.d.). In 2016 alone, the course was taken by over 19,000 people around the world (UN Women Training Centre 2017d: 12). As argued by Alicia Ziffer of the UN Women Training Centre, the organisation which develops and manages the course:

> The course represents an interesting way to bring users onto the same wavelength and share basics ideas and concepts concerning gender equality, women's empowerment and their relationship to human rights frameworks. Although the course's modules may not cover all learning needs, nor will it in itself be enough to promote all necessary transformative processes for gender mainstreaming, its potential as a tool to promote understanding and familiarise users with basic knowledge on gender should be highlighted. (UN Women Training Centre 2015: 2)

In terms of gender training, a number of advantages can be identified for online training from a pedagogical perspective. For example, wider audiences can be reached. This works in two ways. First, it allows for the participation of women and men who may not be able to travel to attend training courses, whether because of travel costs or accessibility issues. Second, it allows for gender training to reach many more people within an institution for a much lower cost than face-to-face training. In large organisations, online training can be used as a 'first step' in a larger transformative process for both individuals, departments and institutions (see Box 4.1).

Box 4.1: An online course on gender training for universities
The Complutense University, Madrid has over 40,000 staff and 60,000 students. In 2016, the Equality Unit began offering face-to-face gender training courses for academic staff, support staff and students. However, it soon became apparent that—while effective and very highly evaluated—this form of training could only reach a limited proportion of the University population. As such, in 2017 the Equality Unit commissioned an online course in gender equality for all three groups across the University community. By covering basic gender concepts and information in an accessible and interactive manner, the course will be able to reach a broad range of people who may not otherwise explicitly engage with issues of gender equality in their daily work or student experiences.

Further potential advantages include that identified by Yang et al.'s (2011) research with university students, which found that online learning can facilitate equitable participation among learners, notably those who may be intimidated by active participation in face-to-face learning environments. Following this, online environments are more horizontal, and the challenges of dominance by particular groups or individuals are mitigated compared to face-to-face training scenarios. In addition, as argued by Kristy Kelly in the 2015 UN Women Training Centre Virtual Dialogue:

> In face to face settings, those people with more education and who can better articulate themselves are more privileged. However, online spaces require more written communication and therefore a literacy that fits an online spaces tend to get privileged. It is also an English language dominated space, but online settings can also overcome this as non-native speakers have more time to contribute. (UN Women Training Centre 2015: 3)

Such findings were echoed by the UN Women Training Centre's *Compendium of Good Practices*, which found that in both the featured experiences of online training—Promundo's PEGE programme and Mupan's online training—"challenges were faced in terms of limited IT knowledge and internet access, especially among older participants or those in more remote/rural areas" (UN Women Training Centre 2016a: 21). This has implications for participatory training that employs feminist principles "as online spaces may ultimately exclude those who lack internet access or IT proficiency, or who do not speak the languages which dominant online platforms" like women's groups in rural areas (ibid.). Nonetheless, Research by SIPA indicates that online trainings are considered more convenient as they are "easily accessible with minimum equipment requirements, normally just a computer and internet connection." In addition to their accessibility, part of their convenience also lies in their cost-effectiveness, as they preclude the "high cost of traveling to face-to-face training sites," thus accommodating budget constraints. Moreover, they allow trainers to "reach populations that would otherwise be excluded from such training opportunities, such as women who are unable to leave their families to travel for a face-to-face opportunity" (Baldursdottir et al. 2014: 30–31).

Moreover, there are also some key challenges in implementing feminist pedagogical principles in online training. As Kirkup et al. (2010: 256) argue, "neither the justifications made for state investment in e-learning in Europe nor most e-learning activities themselves are informed by critical thinking about feminist pedagogy or feminist theory." Specific challenges identified in the literature include the difficulties of inspiring activism and institutional change in online learning environments. As Lai and Lu (2009) found, the geographical and time-based dispersion of students precluded students organising to "apply their newly constructed knowledge or critical voice to advocate issues important to the lives of women today." Where such activities did occur, they tended to be "based on individual effort" and were "unlikely to achieve large-scale social change" (ibid. 2009: 65). Other research suggests that training participants who are highly resistant to gender equality will often be challenged more effectively by a face-to-face than an online course (Lawrence 2013).

General guidelines for good practice in online training are widely available. However, to date, there has been no systematic review of good practices in feminist approaches to online gender training. As such, there are no clear guidelines for applying the feminist pedagogical principles set out above in online settings. The sharing of practices and experiences through events such as the UN Women Training Centre Virtual Dialogue on Online and Mobile Training (2015d) is one example of the development of feminist approaches to online training. Nevertheless, to date there has been very little substantive research on the process or outcomes of online gender training. This remains a key priority for future studies in this field, especially given the growth of online gender training. As argued above, despite the challenges of online training, the potential advantages of this format make it a necessary tool for broader transformative change projects. However, the same conditions to contribute to such change apply to online training as they do across the whole field. Indeed, as argued throughout the book—that gender training must be a part of broader gender equality programmes, processes and strategies in order to have an impact—so online training must be situated within a broader capacity development strategy, for example some face-to-face training and other learning opportunities beyond the online course. Thus, it is argued that "online training should be considered as the first step in a larger transformative process" (Baldursdottir et al. 2014: 37–38). Otherwise, its impact will be limited. The challenge for theorists and practitioners of gender training is to develop models of online training that adhere as closely as possible to feminist pedagogical principles and maximise the potential for such courses to contribute to broader change processes.

Tools and Techniques for Gender Trainers

How, then, can gender trainers navigate the challenges and opportunities of putting feminist pedagogical principles into practice in their (our) work? This question can be approached in two key ways—in terms of tools and techniques, and more broadly in terms of the particular skills and qualities that might make a feminist gender trainer, recalling the discussions on professionalisation and quality standards in Chapter 1. In terms of the former, there is a proliferation of toolkits and manuals for gender training (see, for instance, UN Women Training Centre 2018). However, in a review of training manuals for gender equality in security sector reform, for example, Prügl (2010) finds a focus on conveying instrumental knowledge and technocratic skills. This "pedagogically and methodologically construct trainees as fixed targets in need of knowledge about standards, codes of conduct and reporting mechanisms; and trainers as conduits of that knowledge" (ibid.). Nevertheless, a number of manuals can be identified that engage specifically with gender training from a feminist pedagogical perspective, to a greater or lesser degree, such as those developed by UN Women Training Centre, Oxfam, World Vision and UNESCO. Inspiration can also be drawn from compilations of good practices in the field of training, such as the UN Women Training Centre's (2016a: 21) *Compendium of Good Practices in Training for Gender Equality*, which sheds light on useful methods, strategies and approaches for training initiatives.[1] For instance, its analysis of ten good practice cases provides detailed examples of useful tools, training activities and exercises employed by gender trainers in the field across a range of countries. These tend to place an explicit focus on participatory learning and the validation of personal experience, both principles at the heart of feminist pedagogies. Most recently, the International Training Centre of the International Labour Organization (ITC-ILO) has produced a *Training for Gender Equality Toolkit*, developed for a certification programme for UN staff. This toolkit was developed in a participatory manner at the ITC-ILO's Gender Academy in Turin in November 2017, and showcases a range of methods and activities for gender training with a specific focus on feminist pedagogical principles. This serves as a useful template for developing activities and tools for gender training, as it explicitly encourages reflection on these principles in the design, development and implementation process.

Drawing on these existing materials, a number of key issues can be highlighted for each pedagogical principle in terms of tools and methods for gender training. In terms of *participation*, trainers need to work to play the role of feminist pedagogue and cultivate a feminist classroom. This involves playing a dual role of both facilitator and learner, operating within more "nuanced, grounded, iterative and relationship-oriented understandings" (Mukhopadhyay and Wong 2007) of processes of knowledge transfer. A concrete example of this is the notion of a 'circulation of knowledge', employed by the NGO Promundo and UNFPA, outlined in the UN Women Training Centre's *Compendium of Good Practices*.

[1] Other gender training manuals cover specific sectoral areas or issues, such as the Environment and Energy (UNDP), Gender-based Violence (Restless Development) or Gender and Climate Change (Global Gender and Climate Alliance).

This involved training participants constructing knowledge alongside trainers/facilitators, rather than the transfer of information from trainer to trainee. The trainers:

> facilitated this process, drawing out critical reflections by digging deeper into the 'whys' behind gender, power, privilege and equality. Taking participants out of their comfort zones in this way was a key part of the approach in order to prompt deeper contemplation. Examining power relations, and how these intersect with [intersectional characteristics like] gender, race, sexual orientation, socio-economic status, and age, etc. was considered the key first step in understanding why and how to change unequal gender norms. (UN Women Training Centre 2016a: 63)

In practical terms, constructing a feminist classroom involves both pedagogical and practical aspects, such as the organisation of the learning space and collectively developing expectations with participants early in the session. In the case of online training, it is important to pay particular attention to ensuring active participation and engagement with the materials and activities (Kirkup et al. 2010). As argued above, more specific research and practice needs to be done on 'feminist online classrooms', in order to maximise the transformative potential of all gender training modalities.

Techniques for the *validation of personal experience* in gender training include drawing on participants' existing knowledge on gender and exploring how this relates to the gender equality concepts and skills to be learned in the training. As Marx Ferree (2015: 10–11) argues:

> Learners are not simply "empty mugs" awaiting new and better knowledge from the "jug" of formal gender expertise; instead, training works best when it acknowledges its role in encouraging and supporting contestation over the power of discourse in the existing social relations.

This is highly important in online learning environments, which should respect experience-based knowledge and encourage students to situate and apply knowledge in a way that is personally meaningful and relevant. As discussed above, challenges often arise in gender training scenarios when the personal experiences or beliefs of participants come into tension with ideas—both of the trainer and from feminist theories—about gender equality and transformative change. Tools for addressing this include the trainer acknowledging their own biases and positionality—as practiced by Yellow Window in their trainings. For instance, as described in the *Compendium of Good Practices,* Yellow Window's trainers explicitly acknowledged that "trainers, like all individuals, view reality subjectively, filtering it through the lens of their own biases," particularly shaped by the fact that gender trainers are often women and feminists. Thus, they sought to address their own biases as trainers and use this positionality in the training, on the understanding that, "If a trainer admits to and illustrates [his/]her bias, [both the] trainer and trainee step out of an oppositional relationship and chances are higher trainees will also start to recognise their own biases" (UN Women Training Centre 2016a: 84). In such ways, participants can be encouraged to explore their biases and blindness in relation to gender, in order to make these visible and open to deliberation.

As outlined above, encouraging *social justice, activism and accountability* and *developing critical thinking and open-mindedness* can sometimes come into tension with a technical approach to gender training. That is, trainers may find themselves under pressure to deliver technical content due to limited terms of references, timescales or learning objectives set by the commissioning institution. Such situations require skilful navigation of the limitations of the training scenario in order to maximise its potential as a 'transformative moment', as discussed in more detail in Chapter 5. Tools for encouraging social justice, activism and accountability include, for instance, promoting collective action. An example of this is the approach adopted by organisations like Agribusiness Systems International (ASI) in India or DIMA-COMIBOL in Bolivia—both outlined in the *Compendium of Good Practices.* ASI organised trainees into collective groups to enable them to "overcome the gender-based inequalities and discrimination they face as individuals," while DIMA-COMIBOL equipped participants to become groups of community reporters (UN Women Training Centre 2016a).

An explicit focus on gender equality as political—and on gender training as a political act—can help to make gender training scenarios less technocratic. Participants can be supported to identify the gendered power dynamics at work within an institution and to collectively develop solutions to overcome resistances to change. An example of such an activity is the 'wall of resistances' featured in the ITC-ILO Toolkit (2018, forthcoming), which allows for critical thinking and encourages participants to take responsibility for addressing barriers to transformative change. This relates to Marx Ferree's Knowledge, Desire and Ability (KDA) system. As discussed at length in Chapter 3, this KDA approach holds that gender training is most likely to evoke change if it increases *knowledge*, the *desire* to learn and the *ability* or advocacy skills to apply this learning in practice and access different networks of knowers to challenge gender norms (UN Women Training Centre 2017b). Practical steps include asking participants to produce a Gender Equality Plan at the end of the training and to follow up on this at regular intervals. It is also useful to create a cadre of 'gender advocates' within an organisation, who can work together to promote transformative change beyond the life of a single training initiative. In online training scenarios, this can be encouraged by developing a 'buddy system', in which participants work with a colleague to discuss the key issues raised in the online training and how to address these within their institution.

In terms of *critical thinking*, this involves allowing space for ambiguity within the gender training scenario. Commissioners—and, to a lesser extent, participants—often demand specific skills and outputs from gender training, for example, how to fill in the 'gender form' or how to include gender in existing processes and systems and policies. These skills tend to be returned persistently when theoretical or analytical discussions are raised during the training. The work of the trainer here is to resist 'easy answers' and facilitate an atmosphere of critical thinking and open-mindedness while also conveying the necessary content or skills required to meet the training's learning objectives. In order to address this, for example, Yellow Window employs an 'action learning' approach, in which group learning exercises involve participants engaging with one another and reflecting critically on the training materials in an interactive manner. For instance, alongside group exercises, participants are invited to discuss their own research projects and how gender issues relate to these, before debating these with fellow training participants. This allows them to reflect on the ways in which gender issues relate to their own projects and specific work experiences (UN Women Training Centre 2017c: 84). What such examples demonstrate is that even within a limited curriculum and timeframe, participants can be encouraged to think critically and take responsibility for gender equality within their respective institutions. This is an important insight for overcoming the critiques of gender training, as discussed in Chapter 2.

The Making of a Feminist Gender Trainer

The importance of the trainer's role in gender training is widely acknowledged. For instance, as Alicia Ziffer of the UN Women Training Centre has argued, "the trainer is either the best or worst thing within a training. The trainer is an artist able to readapt and respond to what happens during the training" (UN Women Training Centre 2016a: 21). As argued throughout this book and identified across the literature, one key concern about quality in much gender training, particularly relevant for gender trainers, is that such training is often 'non-feminist' or even anti-feminist in nature. This raises a number of questions for consideration here. As I have asked elsewhere:

> How can we make a claim that someone else's knowledge on gender is wrong – that is, not feminist – and therefore not a true gender approach? Are we saying that only feminists can have gender expertise and knowledge? What, if anything, do we gain for our profession by doing so? (Ferguson 2015)

Drawing from this, how do we—as gender trainers and those concerned with gender training—approach the issue of gender trainers who do not identify as feminist? Should all gender training be feminist? Does this need to be explicit, or can it be implicit? How do we tackle the ways in which institutional cultures may shape and influence trainers in non-feminist ways? Following on from this, apart from employing the tools and methods outlined above, what makes a 'good' gender trainer? What makes a feminist gender trainer? What makes an excellent feminist gender trainer?

As discussed in Chapter 1, there are currently no widely agreed quality criteria or definitions for gender training, and to date there have been limited attempts at professionalisation in the field. In addition, as discussed, these efforts are potentially problematic for a number of reasons. An important issue to acknowledge here is the dependence of trainers on the institutions which commission gender training. The marketisation of gender training "not only tends to shape what gender training looks like; it also makes the tools and methodological approaches developed by trainers a competitive matter, as trainers need to sell their competences on a developing market" (OPERA Team 2011: 55). Moreover, this dependence can limit the freedom and autonomy of trainers to apply an externally imposed set of quality criteria. How might this affect the 'feminist' commitments of trainers and how can this be addressed? Perhaps, a notion of 'minimum standards' and a commitment to flexibility are necessary, to avoid excluding certain groups of actors.

Thus, in crafting an ever more transformative field of feminist gender training, I believe it is useful to have some ideas about what might make a feminist gender trainer. A number of sources can be drawn on here in order to develop this idea further. In the Introduction to KIT's *Revisiting Gender Training*, Mukhopadhyay and Wong (2007: 13) argue that trainers should not take on the role of persuading actors, but rather operate within more "nuanced, grounded, iterative and relationship-oriented understandings" of processes of knowledge transfer. This is very astute, as often in gender training scenarios the role of gender trainer can be reduced to that of a 'persuading actor'. If we accept that we need to move beyond *persuasion*, what other roles might trainers play in the training scenario? In their paper on the professionalisation of gender trainers, Wong et al. (2016: 10) suggest that:

> The role of trainers is to make gender concepts intelligible for participants, in part from relating to practice, without overly simplifying concepts to the point they lose their analytical power. Ideas and concepts need to be presented and understood in ways that development practitioners can use them in order to inform practice. This requires trainers to possess a level of 'fluency' [...] with gender concepts to such a degree that that have a repertoire of ways and examples to make ideas meaningful and relevant to trainees while maintaining their political and analytical power.

They expand their notion of learning a language as a metaphor for gender training, developed by KIT for Plan International's gender equality and child rights capacity building programme, *Planting Equality: Getting it right for Girls and Boys*:

> As gender training facilitators, they are required to be fluent [...] in gender concepts before they start to train others. They need to understand their meanings but know how to use them in different situations, how to communicate their meaning and usage, and how to facilitate learning processes that help others to become fluent. Importantly, becoming 'fluent', whether in a language or gender analysis, should also be inspiring, build confidence and lead to new insights. The role of facilitator is to create a process that critically challenges, generates interest and motivates learners to seek further knowledge and understanding. (Wong et al. 2016: 11)

A more prescriptive approach to quality is set out in UN Women Training Centre's Working Paper on quality. It proposes six criteria for an 'excellent' gender trainer, discussed in turn below. First, drawing on the work of Marx Ferree, the suggestion is that gender trainers need *grounded, situated knowledge and expertise.* That is:

> Trainers can be more or less specialized in specific types of interventions, but the expertise on which they draw is not purely textbook knowledge but rather development of concerted knowledge, motivations and skills through hands-on learning guided by theory. Both a theory of gender that conceptualizes the goals of gender equality and women's empowerment in concrete but generalizable terms and a theory of change that defines what specific training interventions can realistically be expected to accomplish are essential parts of the expertise of trainers, as are pedagogical techniques and vernacularized practice in analyzing organizations, assessing power relations, and identifying potentials for change in specific settings. (Marx Ferree 2015: 26)

This echoes Wong et al. (2016) notion of 'gender fluency' and the metaphor of gender as a language. However, as argued further, gender knowledge also needs to be accompanied by *context-appropriate specialist knowledge, experience and skills.* This may be related to the subject area of the training participants, the type of organisation or the specific regional/national/local context of the training. Best practice in this area suggests that the use of local facilitators is important for overcoming the links between contemporary gender training and postcolonial politics (UN Women Training Centre 2016a: 21), as discussed in Chapter 2. However, it is important to note that both the first and second types of situated knowledge—that is, knowledge gender and the specific context of the training—are important. In some cases, this may require two trainers with different types of knowledge in order to ensure that all aspects of the learning objectives can be adequately met.

The third point proposed by the UN Women Training Centre is the *skilful management of power, resistances and hierarchies.* They refer to Baer et al. (n.d.) notion of 'transformative courage', in which trainers need to encourage resistances and be able to deal with them in order to make them fruitful for the learning of participants. Following Vouhé (2007: 67–68), trainers with a background in social transformation may be particularly well placed to "make participants aware of the path that their professional and private lives are taking as a result of their gender identity, of their choice of values, and of their levels of awareness of different preconceptions about women, men, their images, their roles, and their relationships." This relates to the fourth aspect of quality criteria for gender trainers—to be *skilled in feminist pedagogical practices*, as discussed extensively in this chapter. Wong et al. (2016: 8) acknowledge some of the challenges involved in this. They liken gender training to 'performance':

> Trainers are judged by participants not only for what they are supposed to know but how they share this knowledge in appealing and entertaining ways. Additionally, they are, on the one hand, expected to have expert knowledge, and, on the other, be able to facilitate participants' knowledge deepening. They often face the dual criticism of not knowing enough, because of their emphasis on facilitation, or know too much in the way they present knowledge.

As such, trainers need to tread a careful line between knowledge and facilitation, while acknowledging the performative aspect of their role. I touch on these ideas more explicitly in Chapter 5. The UN Women Training Centre also proposes that gender trainers should *adopt an intersectional approach and analysis*, as discussed throughout this book. This implies a third set of knowledge and expertise—in addition to gender and subject/location-specific knowledge—on intersectional theories. Moreover, as Baer et al. (n.d.), argue, gender trainers need to know how to apply an intersectional perspective to a particular institution and context. It is debatable how many gender trainers currently operating in the field possess these three overlapping sets of expertise and skills, which sets the bar high for excellence in gender training. As such, these knowledge sets can be viewed as a work in progress, which leads on to the final aspect of quality for gender trainers—a commitment to *continual learning, reflexivity and peer review*. As Marx Ferree (2015: 25) argues, "trainers should be viewed as professionals whose judgment, peer networks and continued processes of learning from experience and responding to changes of circumstance are the guarantors of the quality of their work." This is echoed in the Madrid Declaration, which suggests that "reflexivity enhancing practices should be an integral part of any gender + training and mainstreaming proposal and activity, using methods such as questioning, peer review, and intervision" (QUING 2011).

Drawing on this point, this means that while trainers may lack specific knowledge in one of the three areas, a reflexive approach and a commitment to learning can support the development of trainers' knowledge and skills in other areas.

For the purposes of this book, I contend that the qualities and skills proposed by the UN Women Training Centre are desirable for excellent gender trainers. However, speaking more explicitly about *feminist* gender trainers, this approach lacks an understanding of some of the more intangible and complex aspects of gender training, as discussed in more detail in Chapter 5. Kunz's (2016) work is helpful in understanding what these might be. For example, she highlights the importance of openness on the part of the trainer to opportunities for mutual learning and self-questioning, and explores "alternative ways of interaction that attempt to resist the colonial impulse of changing the other" (Kunz 2016: 150–151). Her notion of *encounters* offers a possibility for "a possibility for mutual learning and self-questioning for both gender advisors and researchers, despite constraining structural power differences" (ibid.). This is an interesting framing for gender training scenarios and will be addressed more substantively in the final chapter of this book.

Conclusions

As argued throughout the book, in order to have *transformative* outcomes, gender training needs to be grounded in feminist theory and practice. This chapter has explored feminist pedagogical principles and how these can be applied to gender training scenarios. A number of themes can be identified here in terms of the challenges for gender trainers: first, how to navigate the tensions between 'personal experience' and feminist politics and ideas; second, how to translate feminist pedagogical principles in an online training environment, a field which remains, to date, relatively under-researched in gender training; third, the potential contradictions that arise between feminist gender training and technocratic scenarios in which participants are required to 'tick the gender box' in their own work. The chapter offers some tools and techniques for dealing with these challenges, drawing extensively on the practitioner literature on gender training. In addition, it explores what kinds of qualities and skills might be required for being a *feminist gender trainer*, and an excellent/good trainer more broadly.

What the discussions in this chapter demonstrate is that there are many unresolved and unfinished issues within the field of gender training, especially when it comes to implementing feminist pedagogical principles. At times, training scenarios can be limiting, hostile and technocratic, and the objectives of those commissioning and participating in the training often come into direct conflict with those of the trainers. As highlighted here, a number of under-developed concepts are useful for moving these debates forward. These include Baer et al. (n.d.) notion of 'transformative courage', the idea of gender training as performance (Wong et al. 2016) and gender training as a series of 'encounters' (Kunz 2016). The final chapter of this book explores some of these unresolved issues and tensions in more detail, with a view to increasing the transformative potential of gender training.

References

Baer, S., Keim, J., & Nowottnick, L. (n.d.). *Intersectionality in Gender+ Training*. QUING: Quality in Gender+Equality Policies Integrated Project. Available at: http://www.quing.eu/files/WHY/baer_keim_nowottnick.pdf.

Baldursdottir, M., Fuentes, C., Lianidou, T., Mccrimmon, T., & Qu, Y. (2014). New Approaches to Training for Gender Equality: UN Women Training Centre. Workshop in Development Practice. Sipa Final Report. UN Women and Columbia University's School of International and Public Affairs (SIPA).

Berila, B. (2016). *Integrating Mindfulness into Anti-oppression Pedagogy: Social Justice in Higher Education*. New York and London: Routledge.

Ellsworth, E. (1989). Why Doesn't This Feel Empowering? Working Through the Repressive Myths of Critical Pedagogy. *Harvard Educational Review, 59*(3), 297–325.

Ferguson, L. (2015). 'This Is Our Gender Person': The Messy Business of Working as a Gender Expert in International Development. *International Feminist Journal of Politics, 17*(3), 380–397.

Flood, M. (2011). Men as Students and Teachers of Feminist Scholarship. *Men and Masculinities, 14*(2), 135–154.

Freire, P., & Shore, I. (1987). *A Pedagogy for Liberation: Dialogues on Transforming Education*. Westport, CT and London: Bergin & Garvey.

Gajjala, R., Rybas, N., & Zhang, Y. (2010). Chapter 21: Producing Digitally Mediated Environments as Sites for Critical Feminist Pedagogy. In D. L. Fassett & J. T. Warren (Eds.), *The Sage Handbook of Communication and Instruction*. Thousand Oaks, CA: Sage.

Haraway, D. (1991). *Simians, Cyborgs and Women: The Reinvention of Nature*. New York: Routledge.

Hoffman, F. L., & Stake, J. E. (2001). Feminist Pedagogy in Theory and Practice: An Empirical Investigation. *NWSA Journal, 19*, 79–97.

hooks, b. (1994). *Teaching to Transgress: Education as the Practice of Freedom.* New York: Routledge.

ITC-ILO. (2018, forthcoming). *Training for Gender Equality Toolkit.* Turin: ITC-ILO.

Jackson, P. T. (2016). Safe Spaces and Hospitable Classrooms. *Relations International.* Available at: http://relationsinternational.com/safe-spaces-hospitable-classrooms.

Janus, M. (n.d.). *Feminist Pedagogy.* Available at: http://www.case.edu/artsci/engl/emmons/writing/pedagogy/feminist.pdf.

Kelly, K. (2015). *Social Learning, Adult Learning and Feminist Pedagogies.* Santo Domingo: UN Women Training Centre.

Kirkup, G., Schmitz, S., Kotkamp, E., Rommes, E., & Hiltunen, A. M. (2010). Towards a Feminist Manifesto for E-Learning: Principles to Inform Practices. In S. Booth, S. Goodman & G. Kirkup (Eds.), *Gender Issues in Learning and Working with Information Technology: Social Constructs and Cultural Contexts.* Hershey, PA: Information Science Reference. Available at: http://www.irma-international.org/viewtitle/42500.

Kunz, R. (2016). Windows of Opportunity, Trojan Horses, and Waves of Women on the Move: De-colonizing the Circulation of Feminist Knowledges Through Metaphors? In M. Bustelo, L. Ferguson, & M. Forest (Eds.), *The Politics of Feminist Knowledge Transfer: Gender Training and Gender Expertise* (pp. 99–117). Basingstoke and New York: Palgrave Macmillan.

Lai, A., & Lu, L. (2009). Integrating Feminist Pedagogy with Online Teaching: Facilitating Critiques of Patriarchal Visual Culture. *Visual Culture & Gender.* Available at: http://vcg.emitto.net/4vol/Lai_Lu.pdf.

Lawrence, J. (2013). *Equality and Diversity Training—Online or Face to Face?* Available at: http://www.in-equilibrium.co.uk/equality-and-diversity-training-online-or-face-to-face.

Lombardo, E., & Mergaert, L. (2016). Resistance in Gender Training and Mainstreaming Processes. In M. Bustelo, L. Ferguson, & M. Forest (Eds.), *The Politics of Feminist Knowledge Transfer: Gender Training and Gender Expertise* (pp. 43–61). Abingdon and New York: Palgrave Macmillan.

Manicom, A. (1992). Feminist Pedagogy: Transformations, Standpoints, and Politics. *Canadian Journal of Education, 17*(3), 366–367. Available at: http://www.csse-scee.ca/CJE/Articles/FullText/CJE17-3/CJE17-3-07Manicom.pdf.

Martel, A., & Peterat, L. (1988). Feminist Pedagogies: From Pedagogic Romanticism to the Success of Authenticity. In P. Tancred-Sheriff (Ed.), *Feminist Research: Prospect and Retrospect.* Montreal: Canadian Research Institute for the Advancement of Women.

Marx Ferree, M. (2015). *Training for Gender Equality as a Source of Organisational Change*. Santo Domingo: UN Women Training Centre.

Miller, A. S. (2005). Feminist Pedagogies: Implications of a Liberative Praxis. In K. O. Wicker, A. S. Miller, & M. W. Dube (Eds.), *Feminism New Testament Studies: Global and Future Perspectives*. New York: Routledge.

Mukhopadhyay, M., & F. Wong. (2007). Introduction: Revisiting Gender Training. The Making and Remaking of Gender Knowledge. *Revisiting Gender Training: The Making and Remaking of Gender Knowledge—A Global Sourcebook*. Amsterdam, The Netherlands: KIT Royal Tropical Institute.

OPERA Team. (2011). OPERA Final Report: Advancing Gender+Training in Theory and Practice. Prepared by L. Ferguson & M. Forest. QUING: Quality in Gender+Equality Policies. Available at: http://www.quing.eu/files/results/final_opera_report.pdf.

Palmer, P. J. (1993). *To Know as We Are Known: Education as a Spiritual Journey*. San Francisco: Harper & Row.

Penn, M. (1997). *Feminist Pedagogy as Praxis*. Available at: http://scholarship.law.duke.edu/cgi/viewcontent.cgi?article=1011&context=djglp.

Prügl, E. (2010, October). Gender Expertise and Feminist Knowledge. Presented at the Conference on *Gender Politics in International Governance* (pp. 6–8). Geneva: Graduate Institute.

QUING. (2011, February). Madrid Declaration on Advancing Gender+Training in Theory and Practice (pp. 3–4). Madrid: Complutense University. Available at: http://www.quing.eu/files/madrid_declaration.pdf.

Rajani, L. (2015). *Feminist Pedagogy in University Classroom: Understanding the Classroom as a Place Where Knowledge is Created as Opposed to Knowledge Being Delivered to Students*. Paper presented at the 2015 Hawaii University International Conferences. Available at: http://www.huichawaii.org/assets/lata,-rajani—2015-ahse-huic.pdf.

Sanchez-Casal, S., & MacDonald A. (2002). Introduction: Feminist Reflections on the Pedagogical Relevance of Identity. In S. Sanchez-Casal, S. &A. Macdonald (Eds.), *Twenty-first Century Feminist Classrooms: Pedagogies of Identity and Difference*. New York: Palgrave.

Stanley-Spaeth, B. (2000). *Taming Talos: Cyberfeminist Pedagogy in Classical Studies*. Available at: http://www.tulane.edu/~spaeth/talosabstract.htm.

UN Women Training Centre. (2015). *Virtual Dialogue on Online and Mobile Training for Gender Equality*. Available at: https://trainingcentre.unwomen.org/mod/page/view.php?id=2009.

UN Women Training Centre. (2016a). *Compendium of Good Practices in Training for Gender Equality*. Santo Domingo: UN Women Training Centre. Available at: https://trainingcentre.unwomen.org/pluginfile.php/72/mod_data/content/26773/COMPENDIO_ONU-M-WEB.pdf.

UN Women Training Centre. (2016b). *Typology on Training for Gender Equality*. Santo Domingo: UN Women Training Centre. Available at:

http://www.unwomen.org/en/digital-library/publications/2016/5/typology-on-training-for-gender-equality.

UN Women Training Centre. (2017a). *Working Paper Series: Feminist Pedagogies in Training for Gender Equality*. Prepared by Dr. Lucy Ferguson. Santo Domingo: UN Women Training Centre. Available at: https://trainingcentre.unwomen.org/pluginfile.php/72/mod_data/content/40218/02%20Feminist%20Pedagogies%20.pdf.

UN Women Training Centre. (2017b). *Working Paper Series: A Theory of Change for Training for Gender Equality*. Prepared by Dr. Lucy Ferguson. Santo Domingo: UN Women Training Centre. Available at: https://trainingcentre.unwomen.org/pluginfile.php/72/mod_data/content/40218/01%20Theory%20of%20Change.pdf.

UN Women Training Centre. (2017c). *Working Paper Series: Education and Training for Gender Equality*. Prepared by Dr. Lucy Ferguson. Santo Domingo: UN Women Training Centre. Available at: https://trainingcentre.unwomen.org/pluginfile.php/72/mod_data/content/40218/04%20Education%20vs%20Training.pdf.

UN Women Training Centre. (2017d). *Annual Report 2016*. Santo Domingo: UN Women Training Centre. Available at: http://www.unwomen.org/en/digital-library/publications/2015/9/training-centre-annual-report.

UN Women Training Centre. (2018). *Community of Practice: Resource Library*. Santo Domingo: UN Women Training Centre. Available at: https://trainingcentre.unwomen.org/mod/data/view.php?id=2001.

UN Women Training Centre. (n.d.). *I Know Gender: An Introduction to Gender Equality for UN staff*. Available at: https://trainingcentre.unwomen.org/course/description.php?id=2&lang=en.

Underiner, T. L. (2000). Beyond Recognition, Beholden: Toward a Pedagogy of Privilege. *Signs, 25*(4), 1293–1298.

Vouhé, C. (2007). Gender and Development Training in the Francophone World. In M. Mukhopadhyay & F. Wong (Eds.), *Revisiting Gender Training: The Making and Remaking of Gender Knowledge*. Amsterdam: The Royal Tropical Institute (KIT).

Wicker, K. O., Miller, S., & Dube, M. W. (2005). *Feminist New Testament Studies: Global and Future Perspectives*. New York: Palgrave Macmillan.

Wong, F., Vaast, C., & Mukhopadhyay, M. (2016). *Review and Mapping Exercise for Conceptualizing Professional Development of Gender Trainers: A Working Paper developed for UN Women Training Centre and KIT*. Santo Domingo and Amsterdam: UN Women Training Centre and The Royal Tropical Institute (KIT).

Yang, Y., Cho, Y. J., Mathew, S., & Worth, S. (2011). College Student Effort Expenditure in Online Versus Face-to-Face Courses: The Role of Gender, Team Learning Orientation, and Sense of Classroom Community. *Journal of Advanced Academics, 22*(4), 619–638.

CHAPTER 5

Future Directions for Feminist Gender Training

Abstract The final chapter of the book sets out a number of priorities that have been identified for 'going deeper' with the field of gender training. First, it is argued that a more substantive approach to working with privilege in gender training needs to be developed. Second, new methodologies can be developed drawing from other fields such as applied theatre in order to encourage creativity, empathy and action among training participants. Finally, the chapter explores feminist ways of being in gender training and how techniques and ideas from meditation and mindfulness can be used to summon up the 'transformative courage' required to construct feminist gender training. This involves approaching gender training through honesty, compassion and a commitment to groundlessness. Taken together, these ideas help move gender training beyond its often technocratic form towards a creative, liberating process with the potential to evoke tangible, lasting transformation across individuals and institutions towards gender equality.

Keywords Privilege · Applied theatre · Transformative courage
Creativity · Liberation

As argued throughout this book, contemporary gender training takes place in a context of both limitations and opportunities. A number of key contradictions or tensions have been outlined in the previous chapters. For example, there are strong critiques of gender training from scholars

L. Ferguson, *Gender Training*, Gender and Politics,
https://doi.org/10.1007/978-3-319-91827-3_5

working from a governmentalities approach. In this conceptualisation, gender training is a form of 'coloniality' of gender, which serves to reinforce neoliberal development patterns and—further—to co-opt feminist politics and practice. Second, as highlighted in Chapter 3, the impact of gender training on transformative change is not well documented or understood. This is particularly challenging as there is no systematic approach to the evaluation of gender training. As such, it is difficult to justify the ways in which gender training contributes to broader change processes. The relationship between gender training and transformative change is further challenged by both individual and institutional resistances, as discussed in Chapters 2 and 3, respectively. Finally, a further overarching tension running through the book involves the challenges for gender trainers to resist the technocratic urge of many institutions, responding to the critique that gender training is a 'normalising technique'.

Despite these ongoing tensions and challenges, this book has sought to emphasise the spaces and opportunities for gender training to make a contribution to transformative change. By drawing on experiences from practice, many instances have been highlighted of the ways in which gender trainers engage with challenges in order to generate change. These include, for example, developing techniques for dealing with resistances (Chapter 2) and constructing a gender-transformative approach to evaluating gender training (Chapter 3). As discussed throughout the book, the best chance for gender training to contribute to transformative change is to explicitly engage with feminist pedagogical principles and practices. Gender training contexts are often limited and problematic—as set out above. However, as argued in Chapter 4, a focus on process, rather than content or specific outcomes, can create the space for gender training to involve 'transformative moments' and 'transformative encounters'. This requires gender trainers to be able to maintain a commitment to feminist politics and practices throughout the training process, including in moments of discomfort or resistances.

While the book has covered the main literature from research and practice on gender training, some aspects of the field have, to date, been under-studied. Three key aspects are worth highlighting here in order to understand what might help to move the field of gender training forward, in increasingly feminist and transformative directions. First, contemporary gender training lacks tools and theories for addressing issues of privilege, particularly in terms of elite training participants who work in international institutions. In a critique of gender training in the field of international development, Cornwall (2016: 75) argues that gender training efforts have been targeted at "people living economically precarious lives, rather than at changing those who inhabit positions of power and privilege, including many of us who work for an in development organisations." While this may not reflect the contours of all gender training scenarios, it nevertheless underscores the foundations of contemporary practice. In addition to working on privilege more substantively with gender training participants, there is a strong need for a more systematic reflection on the relative privileges and marginalisations of gender trainers them(our)selves, which may shift depending on the training context. Second, the methodologies used in gender training have, to date, been drawn from a relatively narrow range of fields. In order to push the boundaries of what can be done in gender training, ideas such as Forum Theatre and other forms of applied theatre can be explored in order to enrich the theory and practice of the field. Third, as discussed in Chapter 4, gender trainers are called upon to summon Baer, Keim, and Nowottnick's (n.d.) notion of 'transformative courage' in order to enhance the potential for such training processes to contribute to change. As yet, there is no clear picture of what kinds of tools gender trainers might call upon to summon such courage, and how this could be applied in gender training scenarios. An interesting avenue to explore here is the potential of mindfulness and meditation teachings to support gender trainers to be courageous and seek transformative moments, despite the personal and psychological challenges this may raise. These three aspects are discussed in turn in this chapter, before turning to some final reflections in the concluding section.

Engaging with Privilege

As discussed in Chapter 4, feminist gender training relies on the theory and practice of feminist pedagogies. However, Cornwall (2016: 77) suggests that "the tools and pedagogical practices used for gender training are not sufficient to engage men in confronting and transforming their own male privilege, questioning their own contributions to sustaining male supremacy and bringing the hazards of patriarchy into clearer view." Theorising privilege relies on a range of different fields—both academic and activist—in particular, anti-racism and intersectional feminist approaches. Much of this work draws on McIntosh's (1988) notion of the 'invisible knapsack' of white male privilege, an early classic in exploring the unearned benefits of different types of privilege. Writing from the field of critical pedagogy, Allen and Rossatto (2009: 165) explore the extent to which the tools of this field can be useful for educating privileged students. They discuss the intense opposition to discussions of privilege by students "who act as representatives of the (relative) oppressor group." In particular, they highlight the concern that critical pedagogy is tied to Freire's 'pedagogy of the oppressed' and therefore needs to be carefully considered when applied to students of privilege. Some of the common characteristics of 'oppressor students' when faced with these discussions include the following: dropping the class; resisting deeper readings of critical reading materials, if they read at all; struggling to 'hear' those they read and consistently denying the existence of the structured, oppressive realities that are the social inheritance of the oppressed. To quote them at length:

> These students have a difficult time understanding why they as (future) educators need to focus on social justice. They hold on to individualistic educational psychologies that privilege positivistic learning techniques or non-critical strategies of self-actualization and "higher-order" thinking skills. They often seem to not understand, or not want to understand, why members of oppressed groups do not simply assimilate to the normative order, and they feel that they have "accommodated" the oppressed as much as they are willing to. They exhibit a multiplicity of behaviors and discourses in attempts to distance themselves from self-reflection, whether at a personal or group definition of 'self'. (Allen and Rossatto 2009: 166)

In order to address these resistances, Allen and Rossatto (2009) propose that students need to understand that they can be simultaneously the oppressor within one totality *and* the oppressed within another. They stress that students should be concerned about both their own oppression and their oppression of others. However, as they note, this is challenging in practice, since people tend to be "closer to a consciousness of their oppressed identities than they are of their oppressor identities. For example, in our experience working-class White men are more likely to embrace a class-based critique of schooling than a race- or gender-based one" (ibid.: 170). They suggest that a 'significant emotional and cognitive experience' is required in order to oppressors to come to a problematised understanding of their oppressor identity (ibid.: 175).

This means revising the attention to 'voice' and placing the student at 'the centre'—as oppressors must work on listening to 'others' and not dominating the discussion. In short, "no easy, comfortable exercises will do when it comes to subverting and dismantling the territories of the oppressor" (ibid.: 177). These insights are particularly useful for working on privilege in feminist gender training.

The validation of personal experience—as discussed in Chapter 4—raises some specific challenges for working on privilege. For example, in many gender training scenarios, participants' 'personal experience' can come into tension with feminist ideas—for example, if participants have not personally experienced gender discrimination. When dealing with privilege in gender training scenarios, as Ellsworth (1989: 314) argues, in many cases "it is not enough simply to agree to differ, or work together across differences." For instance, in adult education settings, situations such as anti-academic attitudes or a lack of respect for women in authority fundamentally undermine the basis for dialogue. Such attitudes are often echoed in gender training scenarios. Tisdell (1998), for example, reflects on her practice as an adult educator, arguing that her goal is

> to create activities that will help participants explore the connection between who they are as individuals and the structural systems of privilege and oppression (such as gender, race, and class) that partially inform how they think, how they teach and learn or construct knowledge on an individual level, and inform what is constructed as the "canon" or "official knowledge base" of a particular field.

Tisdell (1998) goes on to highlight that:

> The positionality (gender, race, class, etc.) of all participants, including my own as the instructor, is very significant to how this happens. As an instructor, I teach not only as a woman, but as a middle class white woman. What does my whiteness, or my femaleness, or my class background, as well as the positionalities of my students, have to do with our teaching and learning together? These questions, along with how to deal with the issue of instructor authority and shared power in the classroom, have been central to my own educational theorizing and practice.

In terms of gender training, this is relevant for opening up discussions with participants on intersectional dynamics across organisations, for example, debates that explore who gets hired as a gender trainer and what roles women of colour play within the organisation. As Cornwall (2016) argues, "if we were to begin to acknowledge our own privilege and recognise our agency and responsibility, we would be in a better position to change the games of gendered power that take place all around us in our own institutions." This allows for a richer discussion of gendered hierarchies and opens up a discussion of intersectionality, which is imperative for engaging the privileged in examining their own positions. In terms of overall approaches to working with privilege, two ideas are key—patriarchy and intersectionality. As Cornwall (2016) points out, it is necessary to make "patriarchal values, attitudes, practices and social arrangements visible." She suggests that the issue of visibility is very much dependent on location and identity, and that "what may be invisible to a straight white North American man of a certain age, however, is certainly not out of view to the women or indeed the men of colour or queer men in spaces that such men frequent" (ibid.). Following this, Cornwall poses two important questions. First, "what is needed to make this play of patriarchy and privilege visible to those who cannot otherwise grasp or see it?" Second, once these are made visible, how can gender trainers work to "'undress' the complexities of intersectional difference, and its entailments?" (ibid.).

In terms of research on privilege in gender training, Enderstein's (2018) work demonstrates a number of innovative ways in which gender trainers approach intersectionality in their work, both as an analytical paradigm and as a practical tool. Julia, for example—one of the gender trainers interviewed by Enderstein—discusses a form of *responsiveness* as a way for working with intersectionality. This involves a "close attention to the composition and interaction to the group itself and the understanding that it is necessary to respond to emergent categories of difference specific to the time and space of the training scenario" (ibid.: 11). While the design of gender training may be based on predetermined categories of differences, in their practical interactions gender trainers are able to apply an approach to intersectionality that "relies on emergent and situated identity categories which are linked to a specific time and place" (ibid.: 12).

Other than these general approaches to working on privilege, a range of tools and exercises are available to be used in feminist gender training scenarios. As discussed in Chapter 2, online gender training is growing rapidly, yet there are currently no clear guidelines or best practices for online feminist pedagogies. These courses present a window of opportunity for engaging participants in a reflection on privilege. Examples for such practice include, for example, online 'privilege tests' or games such as 'Privilege Bingo', followed up with a self-reflection exercise which allows space to reject or dispute the results and outcomes of these tests or games. Videos on privilege can also be used as useful ice-breakers for introducing gender training participants to ideas of privilege without explicitly or overtly challenging them in the opening stages of discussions (see Ferguson, forthcoming, for more details). In terms of face-to-face training, the key activities include the paper basket exercise, in which participants are placed at different ends of the training room and asked to throw a ball of paper into a basket at the front of the room. This is useful as it demonstrates in a simple, visual manner how people start from different levels of privilege. Another example is the privilege walk, as set out in the forthcoming ITC-ILO (2018, forthcoming) *Training for Gender Equality Toolkit*. This allows participants to engage with their own privileges and explore some of the different kinds of discrimination they may have experienced in their lifetime. If done well, these kinds of activities respond to Allen and Rossatto's (2009) rejection of 'easy, comfortable exercises'. By drawing on participants' diverse life experiences, these activities can encourage deep and meaningful reflection on the multiple dimensions of privilege. Cornwall outlines a range of further activities in detail, such as 'deconstructing gender', 'gender lines' and the 'wheel of privilege' (Cornwall 2016, see sections 2.1, 2.2 and 2.3). Beyond this, she highlights more broadly the power of 'telling tales' and includes the example of setting a story-telling task in between training sessions, arguing that:

> Once men who 'just turn up' begin to realise what is going on in the play of power and privilege in the room, their interventions can help to change the dynamics, even and sometimes especially if it involves simply staying silent. (ibid.)

In order to grapple with notions of privilege in gender training scenarios, it is important to understand the multiple dynamics of hierarchies, discrimination and marginalisation that are at play. As argued in Chapter 1, gender training is a diverse and pluralistic endeavour, which engages both trainers and participants from a wide range of socioeconomic and cultural backgrounds. As such, there are no fixed power dynamics of gender training scenarios. Instead, these may be multiple and may shift constantly as the training process develops. In order to facilitate these kinds of discussions on privilege, gender trainers need to be reflexive, as discussed in Chapter 4. This means highlighting the importance of the positionality of the gender trainer in navigating discussions of privilege. As discussed below, this may not always be a comfortable position for gender trainers. Above all, it is an approach that requires skill and courage. However, by opening up a discussion of privileges as plural, changeable and relational, gender trainers are able to work with these issues in a tangible and productive manner. This is important as it helps to use the process of gender training as an opportunity for collectively exploring power dynamics, and working together with participants to see how these can be redressed at the individual, group and institutional levels. Alongside discussions of privileges, it is important to explore new fields—such as applied theatre—from which gender training methodologies are drawn, as discussed in the section below.

Gender Training and Applied Theatre

By looking at lessons learned from the field of applied theatre, it is possible to engage more substantively with some of the dilemmas and challenges discussed throughout the book, particularly in Chapter 4. To date, there has been a small amount of work that aims to bring lessons from theatre and drama into gender training scenarios. Cornwall, for example, details her experiences in using theatre practices to work with patriarchy (2016: 84). Reflecting on these practices, she argues that:

> Sequencing from the liminal play-world of drama into strategising for change gives people a set of reference points that can invite a much more inclusive, and deeper, conversation because of what people are able to see and do. (ibid.)

In another example, *PartecipArte*[1] in Rome works with organisations such as the Food and Agriculture Organization of the United Nations (FAO) and the World Food Programme (WFP) to explore issues such as gender-based violence and masculinities. However, to date, there have been few attempts to explicitly link the methodologies and tools of applied theatre to institutional change for gender equality. This section

[1] http://www.parteciparte.com/en/.

offers a preliminary exploration of what gender training can learn from theatre and what kinds of techniques could be used to support the transformative potential of gender training.

Applied theatre draws largely from the work of Boal (2009) and his *Theatre of the Oppressed*. This involves a focus on the action itself, rather than the actor(s). Rather, it is the 'liberated spectator' who creates the action. While Boal acknowledges that the theatre is not a revolution in itself, he argues that these theatrical forms are without doubt a 'rehearsal of revolution' (Boal 2009: 131). By practicing these forms, spectators/participants are left with "a sort of uneasy sense of incompleteness that seeks fulfilment through real action" (ibid.). Using Boal's notion, how can these forms be adapted into a *rehearsal for gender equality* or a *rehearsal for transformative institutional change*? As Heathcote (2009: 200) argues, drama "does not freeze a moment in time, it freezes a problem in time, and you examine the problem as people go through a process of change." She encourages educators not to fear the use of drama, and that it only demands participants to:

> Think from within a dilemma instead of talking about the dilemma. That's all it is; you bring them to a point where they think from within the framework of choices instead of talking coolly about the framework of choices. You can train people to do this in two minutes, once they are prepared to accept it. (Heathcote 2009: 204)

This is useful for gender training, where much emphasis has been placed on the verbal aspects of exploring gender issues. In contrast, drama generates "the reflective energy that comes out of the experience," which can then be used to explore the possibilities for change. Freire (2009) distinguishes between *cultural invasion*—whose aim is domination—and *cultural synthesis*—whose aim is liberation. In theatrical interventions that work from cultural synthesis, "the actors become integrated with the people, who are co-authors of the action that both perform upon the world," creating a 'climate of creativity' (ibid.: 311). This is useful for gender training, which—as outlined throughout the book and particularly in Chapter 2—has often tended to be delivered in dry and technocratic ways, sidelining creative methodologies in favour of more technical and 'practical' approaches. As argued in Chapter 4, gender training engages with emotions and personal experience, yet currently lacks substantive methods for dealing with these effectively. As Selman et al. (2009: 322) suggest from experience of working with young people on safe sex in schools:

> People involved with theatre for change discuss its power to make issues personal, to reach people on emotional levels, to increase empathy and identification with characters. Greater emotional engagement creates higher stakes; audiences feel that these things matter to people they care about.

How, then, can gender training employ techniques from applied theatre to achieve this greater emotional engagement? And what might be the role of gender trainers in these processes? As quoted in Chapter 4, Wong et al. (2016) have likened gender training to 'performance', in particular the need to share gender knowledge in appealing and entertaining ways. This recalls the role of the 'joker' or 'fool' from theatre. As Prentki (2009a: 253) elaborates:

> The applied theatre facilitator, in the European tradition of the stage fool, is not only adept at crossing borders but also plays along the edges of art and life to expose contradictions and invite reflections upon the theatrical in life and the lively in theatre. In moving from a play to play the foolish facilitator draws participants back into the carnival of the human senses.

In many ways, this expands further on Wong, Vaast and Mukhopadhyay's notion of performance and the 'foolish facilitator', which fits with Selman et al.'s reminder of the importance of laughter and humour in applied theatre, and how these are useful for bringing down people's defences (Selman et al. 2009: 320). In gender training, the trainer/fool/joker can use laughter and humour to help bring down the defences of participants and open them up to the issues being discussed. This is particularly useful for working with those who are in positions of privilege within organisations, as discussed above. As Prenkti (2009b: 182) points out, in applied theatre, often the focus has been on working with the oppressed as opposed to those with those best placed to bring about change. The same is true for gender training. Prenkti cites Henneman's *Teatro di Nascosto* (Hidden Theatre)[2]—in which members of national and European parliaments and relevant professionals recite, verbatim, stories of asylum seekers alongside actors and refugees—as an example of how theatre can be applied to the powerful. In this performance, he (2009b: 183) argues, "the theatrical force of empathy is let loose upon

[2] http://teatrodinascosto.com/en/about.

those who have the power to make and unmake the legal framework." Further reflections from Prenkti are useful in understanding and overcoming some of the resistances—both individual and institutional—discussed in Chapters 2 and 3, respectively. He notes that:

> When working with groups who hold power in particular communities, police, politicians or whomever, it is often the border between the professional and the human being that is the hardest to cross. The prospect of being stripped of the protective shell of the social role can induce fear and evasion among those for whom professional habits have shut off access to the wellsprings of imagination and creativity. The underlying principle in all these various applications of the theatre process is fundamentally the same: to enable the participants to (re)discover their innate capacities for play, for imagining, for creating, for relating to others by exploring the self in the other and the other in the self. (Prenkti 2009b: 252).

Having explored some of the foundational principles of applied theatre and its potential contribution to gender training, what kinds of specific tools and techniques could be operationalised in gender training scenarios? The best known method used in terms of gender equality is 'Forum Theatre' which, at its best, "retains the subversive intentions of its origins, as a counterweight to the standard power relations obtaining in the theatre context, and by extension, in the society which supports that theatre" (Jackson 2009: 41). However, Forum Theatre requires a company of actors and a long stage of development and rehearsal in collaboration with the relevant communities/organisations for which it is performed. As such, for the purposes of more short-term gender training scenarios, a number of more short-term ideas and techniques can be highlighted here. Cornwall (2016: 84–85), for example, describes an activity in which participants in gender training develop and perform 'skits', during which fellow participants can stop the action and explore how things could be done differently, following the principles of Forum Theatre. She argues that it is important to be clear about the purpose of such activities—identifying and working with the 'deep culture' in an organisation. Drawing on her experience in using these techniques for gender training, Cornwall (2016: 85) reflects that:

> Processing these small pieces of theatre can generate a rich seam of reflection on the patriarchal dynamics that are so often viscerally part of organisational culture, even in apparently progressive organisations. From here,

> the discussion can be guided into actions that can be taken – ground-rules, policies, procedures or other forms of institutional intervention that can change the scene.

Other methods for using theatre to reflect on organisational culture include, for example, Weaver's (2009) work with women in prison, in which she explores the 'rhythm' of institutions and how to use this. She works with "portraiture, both real and fantasy, with forms of personal communication, like likes and letters and is rooted in the details of daily life, like laundry and teacups" (ibid.: 56). It would be interesting to explore the equivalent to 'laundry and teacups' in the daily life of organisations in which gender training takes place, while adapting and translating Weaver's exercises with prisoners for gender training scenarios. How could a 'narrative approach' be incorporated into gender training techniques, and what kinds of activities could be developed to facilitate this? Further ideas can be drawn directly from Boal's (2009) work. For example, photography is a useful tool for discovering "valid symbols for a whole community or social group" (ibid.: 132). This could be applied in gender training scenarios by asking participants to take photographs with their phones prior to the training—photographs that they believe symbolise aspects of gender in/equality in their organisation or daily lives. These can then be discussed in the opening session of the training. Finally, Image Theatre holds significant potential for adaptation to gender training scenarios. Here the bodies and faces of participants are used to create 'sculptures'—either as individuals or in groups. The key here is that the participant who plays the role of sculptor is not allowed to speak and can only direct fellow participants either by touch or by mime (to be agreed by the group). Following this, participants discuss whether they agree with the representation of the situation via the 'statues'. Once the tableau is accepted by all, each participant is asked to propose ways of changing it. As Boal (2009: 136) argues, "this form of image theatre is without doubt one of the most stimulating, because it is so easy to practice and because of its extraordinary capacity for making thought visible. This happens because use of the language idiom is avoided." As such, techniques such as Image Theatre allow participants to move beyond words and draw on creativity in order to explore gender issues. Such ideas of how gender training can employ techniques from applied theatre to achieve greater emotional, non-verbal engagement are useful to bear in mind as we reflect on feminist 'ways of being' for gender trainers, to which we turn below.

Feminist Ways of Being for Gender Trainers

A recurring theme in terms of challenges for gender trainers is how to cope when gender training scenarios become challenging, contentious or even hostile. As argued throughout the book, resistance is a key part of change processes—both in individual and institutional terms. Engaging with—rather than smothering or minimising—resistances requires sincerity and honesty about losing power and privileges on the part of both trainers and participants, as discussed above. Moreover, resistances to/in gender training need to be dealt with in a way that involves empathy and compassion for training participants and, indeed, for the trainers themselves. The gender trainers interviewed in Enderstein's (2018: 13) study highlight the importance of an 'affective connection' for tackling challenging or sensitive issues with participants. As discussed in Chapter 4, Kunz, for example, highlights the importance of openness on the part of the trainer to opportunities or *encounters* for mutual learning and self-questioning, which offer a possibility for "a possibility for mutual learning and self-questioning for both gender advisors and researchers, despite constraining structural power differences" (2016: 150–151). For Cornwall (2016):

> It is about opening ourselves up to the possibility that others may see, feel and know very differently. And being open, too, to recognising that through this we might all find ourselves in a better place.

These ideas overlap with those of hooks on marginality—"that space in the margin that is a site of creativity and power" (hooks 2009: 85). This notion of 'spaces' offers a complement to the analysis of 'transformative moments' discussed throughout the book. While institutions may be resistant to gendered change, "spaces can be interrupted, appropriated, and transformed through artistic and literary practice" (ibid.: 85).

In addition to the feminist pedagogical principles and practice outlined in Chapter 4, from what other sources can gender trainers draw upon to support themselves in the difficult moments of gender training? How can gender trainers stick with these uncomfortable feelings so that these 'difficult moments' be used to work towards the transformative outcomes that are the key concern of feminist gender training? Again, drawing on applied theatre, Salverson's (2009: 39) work on a theatre that grapples with 'risky stories' is helpful here: "a tenacious, nonsentimental insistence on life within loss that is honest, ready to risk failure, and absolutely courageous." Quoting her colleague Steven Hill, she advises us to "always stay in the shit," as "that is where the humanity and possibilities lie." This is echoed in the discussions in Chapter 4 about resisting easy answers and quick fixes in gender training. This requires an ability to stay in the moment and not look for an exit.

In order to explore this more deeply, gender trainers can draw on the work of meditation teachers. As Chodron (2016: 6) argues, "fear is a natural reaction to moving closer to the truth." She highlights how standing on the edge of the unknown leads to 'groundlessness', through which we "find that the present moment is a pretty vulnerable place and that this can be completely unnerving and completely tender at the same time" (ibid.). The trick, she suggests, is "to keep exploring and not bail out, even when we find out that something is not what we thought" (ibid.: 10). The simple practice of pausing and waiting instead of immediately filling the space—which is already instinctive to the practice of many gender trainers—can be a transformative experience:

> Right then, we can feel that energy, do our best to let the thoughts dissolve, and give ourselves a break. Beyond all that fuss and bother is a big sky. Right there in the middle of the tempest, we can drop it and relax. (ibid.: 47)

Following this, she explores ways to 'get unstuck', suggesting that "what we call obstacles are really the way the world and our entire experience teach us where we're stuck. What may appear to be an arrow or a sword we can actually experience as a flower" (ibid.: 87). This notion of 'experiencing a sword as a flower' is useful for the most challenging aspects of gender training, particularly in contexts of strong resistances and tensions. In order to develop the practice of gender training and to summon the 'transformative courage' required, gender trainers need to be able to "look clearly and compassionately at ourselves" (ibid.: 101). Only then can "we feel confident and fearless about looking into someone else's eyes" (ibid.). Working with these ideas from applied theatre and mindfulness goes beyond a discussion of *reflexivity*—which can remain on the intellectual plane. Rather, they challenge gender trainers to seek ways to work with creativity, courage and groundlessness. The application of these methodologies and approaches is in an early stage, but it is useful to offer some thoughts on how the field can move forward.

Conclusions

This book has explored how to maximise the transformative potential of gender training scenarios and processes. As Kunz and Prügl have argued (forthcoming: 29):

> some gender experts working 'in the field' would prefer a debate and exchange of information rather than the implementation of ready-made projects. Valorizing their innovative practices may provide a venue for feminist scholarship to establish the authority of a distinctly feminist form of gender expertise.

Throughout the book, such 'innovative practices' have been highlighted and interrogated in order to overcome some of the key challenges for gender training—in particular, for *feminist* forms of gender training. Feminist gender training is "reflexive, self-critical and focused on process" and "urges us to focus on the transformative potential of gender training moments and encounters" (Ferguson, forthcoming). Each chapter of the book develops a key argument regarding how such a feminist gender training can be approached and developed. Chapter 1, for example, argues that gender training should be seen as a moment of rupture or disturbance in institutional change processes, which—in the best-case scenario—can be converted into opportunities for transformative change. Chapter 2 sets out the key critiques of gender training from the academic literature, such as the claim that gender training has become a 'normalising technology' (Davids and van Eerdewijk 2016: 87) or that debates over gender inequalities are pushed from the realm of politics into the realm of expertise (Kunz 2016). In response to these critiques, the chapter engages substantively with some of the key challenges of gender training from the perspective of reflexive practice, exploring some of the key issues that stop gender training contributing to transformative change. The key point to highlight here is the need to work strategically within the constraints of gender training processes and scenarios.

Transformative change for gender equality is the key overarching theme of the book. In Chapter 3, the possibilities and limitations of gender training for contributing to such change are explored in detail. The chapter argues for a move beyond a focus on individual change—as demonstrated in current approaches to the evaluation of gender training—and rather on exploring institutional resistances and institutional change. This draws on both academic literature on feminist institutionalism and reflections from practice, with a focus on maximising the impact of gender training on institutional change. A key concern for future work in gender training is the lack of a clearly articulated theory of the relationship between gender training and transformative change. This requires a more substantive analysis of the specific contexts of institutional power dynamics and other change processes, as well as further work on Theory of Change approaches and gender-transformative evaluation of gender training. However, as argued in Chapter 3, even without perfect conditions, gender trainers can work to maximise the spaces for feminist change within existing constraints and conditions. An important aspect of maximising the transformative potential of gender training is the application of feminist pedagogical principles throughout all aspects of the training process. This is explored in detail in Chapter 4, which discusses not just feminist pedagogical principles, but also what makes a *feminist gender trainer.* The chapter also highlights a range of unresolved and unfinished issues within the field of gender training, especially when it comes to implementing feminist pedagogical principles—in particular the tensions between technocratic demands and feminist politics and practice. Feminist gender training will require individual, collective and institutional 'transformative courage' in the face of such challenges.

In this final chapter of the book, a number of priorities have been identified for 'going deeper' with the field of gender training. First, as argued above, a more substantive approach to working with privilege in gender training needs to be developed. Second, new methodologies should be drawn from other fields—such as applied theatre, as highlighted here—in order to move beyond the current set of tools and techniques to encourage creativity, empathy and action among training participants. Following hooks, "we are transformed, individually, collectively, as we make radical creative space which affirms and sustains our subjectivity, which gives us a new location from which to articulate our sense of the world" (2009: 85). Finally, the chapter explores *feminist ways of being* in gender training and how techniques and ideas from meditation and mindfulness can be used to summon up the 'transformative courage' required to construct feminist gender training. This involves approaching gender training through honesty, compassion and a commitment to groundlessness. Above all, the ideas explored in this book aim to enable gender trainers to seek ways to work with creativity, courage and groundlessness. Taken together, these ideas help to move gender training beyond its often technocratic form towards a creative, liberating process with the potential to evoke tangible, lasting transformation across individuals and institutions towards our common goal—gender equality.

References

Allen, R. L., & Rossatto, C. A. (2009). Does Critical Pedagogy Work with Privileged Students? *Teacher Education Quarterly, 36*(Winter), 163–180.

Baer, S., Keim, J., & Nowottnick, L. (n.d.). *Intersectionality in Gender+ Training*. QUING: Quality in Gender+ Equality Policies Integrated Project. Available at http://www.quing.eu/files/WHY/baer_keim_nowottnick.pdf.

Boal, A. (2009). Theatre of the Oppressed. In T. Prentki & S. Preston (Eds.), *The Applied Theatre Reader*. London and New York: Routledge.

Chodron, P. (2016). *When Things Fall Apart: Heart Advice for Difficult Times*. Boulder, CO: Shambhala.

Cornwall, A. (2016). Towards a Pedagogy for the Powerful. *IDS Bulletin, 47*(5). Available at http://bulletin.ids.ac.uk/idsbo/article/view/2801/ONLINE%20ARTICLE.

Davids, T., & van Eerdewijk, A. (2016). The Smothering of Feminist Knowledge: Gender Mainstreaming Articulated Through Neoliberal Governmentalities. In M. Bustelo, L. Ferguson, & M. Forest (Eds.),*The Politics of Feminist Knowledge Transfer: Gender Training and Gender Expertise* (pp. 80–98). Abingdon and New York: Palgrave Macmillan.

Ellsworth, E. (1989). Why Doesn't This Feel Empowering? Working Through the Repressive Myths of Critical Pedagogy. *Harvard Educational Review, 59*(3), 297–325.

Enderstein, A. M. (2018). 'First of All, Gender Is Power': Intersectionality as Praxis in Gender Training. *Studies on Home and Community Science, 11*(2), 44–56.

Ferguson, L. (Forthcoming). *Constructing a 'Pedagogy for the Privileged' in Gender Training*. Paper Presented to *ECPG Conference*, June 2017.

Freire, P. (2009). Pedagogy of the Oppressed. In T. Prentki & S. Preston (Eds.), *The Applied Theatre Reader*. London and New York: Routledge.

Heathcote, D. (2009). Drama as a Process for Change. In T. Prentki & S. Preston (Eds.), *The Applied Theatre Reader*. London and New York: Routledge.

hooks, b. (2009). Choosing the Margin as a Space of Radical Openness. In T. Prentki & S. Preston (Eds.), *The Applied Theatre Reader*. London and New York: Routledge.

ITC-ILO. (2018, forthcoming). *Training for Gender Equality Toolkit.* Turin: ITC-ILO.

Jackson, A. (2009). Provoking Intervention. In T. Prentki & S. Preston (Eds.), *The Applied Theatre Reader.* London and New York: Routledge.

Kunz, R. (2016). Windows of Opportunity, Trojan Horses, and Waves of Women on the Move: De-colonizing the Circulation of Feminist Knowledges Through Metaphors? In M. Bustelo, L. Ferguson, & M. Forest (Eds.), *The Politics of Feminist Knowledge Transfer* (pp. 99–117). Abingdon and New York: Palgrave Macmillan.

Kunz, R., & Prügl, E. (Forthcoming). *Gender Expertise in International Governance: A Conceptual Introduction.* Paper Presented at *ECPG Conference*, Lausanne, June 2016.

McIntosh, P. (1988). White Privilege: Unpacking the Invisible Knapsack. In P. McIntoch (Ed.), *White Privilege and Male Privilege: A Personal Account of Coming to See Correspondences Through Work in Women's Studies.* Wellesley, MA: Wellesley College, Center for Research on Women.

Prentki, T. (2009a). Introduction to Border Crossing. In T. Prentki & S. Preston (Eds.), *The Applied Theatre Reader.* London and New York: Routledge.

Prentki, T. (2009b). Introduction to Intervention. In T. Prentki & S. Preston (Eds.), *The Applied Theatre Reader.* London and New York: Routledge.

Salverson, J. (2009). Clown, Opera, the Atomic Bomb and the Classroom. In T. Prentki & S. Preston (Eds.), *The Applied Theatre Reader.* London and New York: Routledge.

Selman, J., Esmail, S., Munro, B., & Ponzetti, J. (2009). Are We There Yet? On the Road to Safer Sex Through Interactive Theatre. In T. Prentki & S. Preston (Eds.), *The Applied Theatre Reader.* London and New York: Routledge.

Tisdell, E. J. (1998). Poststructural Feminist Pedagogies: The Possibilities and Limitations of Feminist Emancipatory Adult Learning Theory and Practice. *Adult Education Quarterly, 48,* 139–156.

Weaver, L. (2009). Doing Time: A Personal and Practical Account of Making Performance Work in Prisons. In T. Prentki & S. Preston (Eds.), *The Applied Theatre Reader.* London and New York: Routledge.

Wong, F., Vaast, C., & Mukhopadhyay, M. (2016). *Review and Mapping Exercise for Conceptualizing Professional Development of Gender Trainers: A Working Paper Developed for UN Women Training Centre and KIT.* Santo Domingo and Amsterdam, The Netherlands: UN Women Training Centre and the Royal Tropical Institute (KIT).

Index

L. Ferguson, *Gender Training*, Gender and Politics,
https://doi.org/10.1007/978-3-319-91827-3

CPSIA information can be obtained
at www.ICGtesting.com
Printed in the USA
LVHW081800050223
738717LV00010B/1644

9 783319 918266